Energy Efficient Networking Systems and Communication Technologies

Edited by **Tim Kurian**

LANRYE
INTERNATIONAL

New Jersey

Published by Clanrye International,
55 Van Reypen Street,
Jersey City, NJ 07306, USA
www.clanryeinternational.com

Energy Efficient Networking Systems and Communication Technologies
Edited by Tim Kurian

International Standard Book Number: 978-1-63240-208-0 (Hardback)

Printed in the United States of America.

Energy Efficient Networking Systems and Communication Technologies

Contents

Preface   VII

Chapter 1   **Energy Efficient Communication for**
             Underwater Wireless Sensors Networks   1
             Ammar Babiker and Nordin Zakaria

Chapter 2   **Achieving Energy Efficiency in Analogue**
             and Mixed Signal Integrated Circuit Design   25
             E. López-Morillo, F. Márquez, T. Sánchez-Rodríguez,
             C.I. Luján-Martínez and F. Munoz

Chapter 3   **Self-Cancellation of Sampling**
             Frequency Offsets in STBC-OFDM
             Based Cooperative Transmissions   49
             Zhen Gao and Mary Ann Ingram

Chapter 4   **The Energy Efficient Techniques in the DCF of**
             802.11 and DRX Mechanism of LTE-A Networks   71
             Kuo-Chang Ting, Hwang-Cheng Wang, Fang-Chang Kuo,
             Chih-Cheng Tseng and Ping Ho Ting

Chapter 5   **Energy Efficiency of Connected Mobile**
             Platforms in Presence of Background Traffic   103
             Sameh Gobriel, Christian Maciocco
             and Tsung-Yuan Charlie Tai

Chapter 6   **Monitoring Energy Efficiency in Buildings with**
             Wireless Sensor Networks: *NRG-WiSe Building* 117
             I. Foche, M. Chidean, F.J. Simó-Reigadas, I. Mora-Jiménez,
             J.L. Rojo-Álvarez, J. Ramiro-Bargueno and A.J. Caamano

             Permissions

             List of Contributors

Preface

This book provides a descriptive and comprehensive introduction to energy efficient networking systems and communication technologies. Energy efficiency in communication and networking systems is increasingly attracting attention due to both financial and ecological reasons. The amount of power consumed by information and communication technologies (ICT) is speedily growing, as well as the energy bill of service providers. According to many recent researches, ICT single-handedly is accountable for a major chunk of energy consumption which varies from 2% to 10% of the world power utilization. Energy-efficiency is a feature that until recently was only considered for battery determined tools. Nowadays, we see energy-efficiency becoming a persistent issue that will need to be considered in all areas of technology from device technology to systems organization. This book is a compilation of latest research data on hardware design, architectures, protocols and algorithms. This will not only help in making communication devices more energy-efficient but also lead to a future with more infrastructures based on energy-saving technologies.

After months of intensive research and writing, this book is the end result of all who devoted their time and efforts in the initiation and progress of this book. It will surely be a source of reference in enhancing the required knowledge of the new developments in the area. During the course of developing this book, certain measures such as accuracy, authenticity and research focused analytical studies were given preference in order to produce a comprehensive book in the area of study.

This book would not have been possible without the efforts of the authors and the publisher. I extend my sincere thanks to them. Secondly, I express my gratitude to my family and well-wishers. And most importantly, I thank my students for constantly expressing their willingness and curiosity in enhancing their knowledge in the field, which encourages me to take up further research projects for the advancement of the area.

Editor

Energy Efficient Communication for Underwater Wireless Sensors Networks

Ammar Babiker and Nordin Zakaria
PETRONAS University of Technology
Malaysia

1. Introduction

Water covers more than 70% of the planet, contains much of its natural resources, and defines the greater territories of many nations. With the increasing use of underwater sensors for the exploitation and monitoring of vast underwater resources, underwater wireless sensor network (UWSN), mostly based on acoustic transmission technologies, have been developing steadily in terms of operation range and data throughput.

As in terrestrial sensor networks, various data transport protocols have been designed for UWSN (Pompili, 2007). However, as yet, there is no internationally accepted standard for underwater communication. The lack of standard is due to the technical challenges that still persist in establishing reliable underwater wireless data communication. Firstly, in underwater environment, electromagnetic wave is rarely of use, unlike in terrestrial space, as it can only travel a short distances due attenuation and absorptions effects. Optical signal suffers from scattering and absorption in underwater (Akyildiz, et al., 2005). Hence, to date acoustic energy is the most widely used type of signals used in underwater data transmission. Secondly, the fluctuating nature of ocean condition causes high bit error rate in acoustic transmission. Underwater acoustic transmission is also affected by path loss caused by spreading and absorption, noise which comes from many sources like water current, rain, wind, seismic and volcanic activities or biological phenomena (Pompili, 2007). Signal reflection and refraction from the surface and seabed, topographic sources like hills and hollows are some example error sources.

Hence in underwater environment, the two main issues of concern are namely: reliability and energy efficiency. These two issues are inter-twined. Reliability requires error-correction, and error-correction requires energy. More reliability tends to imply higher energy consumption, causing difficulty in applications that require nodes to be operated underwater for long periods of time without batteries recharging, and in aquatic environments that render hard the task of recharging or replacing batteries (Pompili, 2007; Preisig, 2007). Appropriate strategy must therefore be in-place to ensure reliable data transmission, while conserving energy.

In this chapter, we focus on the energy efficiency issue in UWSN. We develop a mathematical model of the efficiency of acoustic data communication in realistic underwater environment. We analyze existing error-correction techniques, and we then propose a new adaptive hybrid error correction technique that improves upon existing techniques.

We organize the rest of this chapter as follows: In section 2, we briefly review the basics of acoustic propagation. In section 3, we review the two most widely used underwater error correction techniques, ARQ and FEC. In section 4, we present mathematical and simulation analysis of the energy efficiency of the techniques. In section 5, an Adaptive Hybrid Energy Efficient Error Correction (AHEC) technique for Underwater Wireless Sensor Networks (UWSN) data transmission is presented. Finally, in section 6, we conclude the chapter.

2. Basics of acoustic propagation

Factors that characterized underwater acoustic propagation include path loss, noise, multipath, Doppler spread, and high and variable propagation delay. Those factors are the main reason for the variability in the acoustic channel. Bandwidth varies from a few KHz in a long range system which operates over several tens of kilometers to more than hundred KHz in a short-range system that operates over several tens of meters. UAC system are classified according to their communication ranges as shown in Table 1 (Akyildiz, et al., 2004, 2005):

	Range (Km)	Bandwidth (KHz)
Very long	1000	<1
Long	10-1000	2-5
Medium	1-10	=10
Short	0.1 -1	20-50
Very short	<0.1	>100

Table 1. Underwater Acoustic Communication System Ranges

Below are the factors that characterize underwater acoustic propagation (Colin et al., 2007; Joshy and Babu, 2010; Stojanovic and Preisig, 2009):

- Path loss: there are two main sources for path losses for underwater acoustic propagation:
  - Attenuation: this is the loss due to the conversion of acoustic energy into heat which known as absorption loss.
  - Spreading: this is the loss due to the expansion of the signal energy over a large area as the wave propagates forward.
- Noise: there are two kind of noise:
  - Man-made noise: it is caused by machinery (pumps, reduction gears, etc), shipping activities, etc.
  - Ambient noise: this is caused by the movement of water which includes tides, current, storms, wind, and rain. It is also caused by biological phenomena. Ambient noise depends mainly on frequency, so it must be considered when selecting frequency band in underwater communications systems (Preisig , 2007).
- Multipath: In most environments, the ocean can be modelled as a wave guide for communication signals. This waveguide is characterized by a reflecting surface and ocean bottom and a variant sound speed. Reflection, refraction and diffraction will occur with those surfaces resulting in multiple propagation paths from the source to the

receiver. Horizontal channel is characterized by long multipath spreads compared with vertical one. A multipath with varying impulse response tends to be subjected to an Inter Symbol Interference (ISI) that causes severe degradation in the acoustic signals.

- High delay and delay variance: underwater acoustic signal speed is just 1500 m/s, which is lower than electromagnetic signal by more than 5 orders of magnitude. The propagation delay is large too (about 0.67s/km).
- Doppler spread: it is significant in underwater acoustic channel, and cause degradation in the performance of digital communications..

Most of the factors mentioned above are caused by the chemical-physical properties of the sea water such as temperature, salinity and density, which these factors vary with depth, space and time.

3. Error correction techniques

Automatic Repeat reQuest (ARQ) and Forward Error Correction (FEC) are two commonly used strategies to combat error in underwater transmission (Bin et al, 2008). ARQ which proposes retransmission (Kunal et al., 2010), are widely used in data communications system for error control as they are simple and provide high reliability. However, the throughput is not constant and decreases rapidly in high bit error rate cases (Lin et al., 1984). In FEC, redundancy is added for error prevention. Redundant bits are encapsulated with data bits to form encoded information. However this increases the payload for transmission. Addition of redundant bit is known as channel coding. Error Correcting Codes (ECC) (block or convolutional) are used for this purpose. FEC codes have constant throughput which is equal to the code rate. However it has the drawback of using parity bit irrespective of the existence of errors. Reliability can be enhanced by combining FEC and ARQ, forming what is known as Hybrid-ARQ (HARQ) (Kunal et al., 2010).

3.1 Automatic repeat request

ARQ uses error detection codes, acknowledgement and/or negative acknowledgement messages, and time out to retransmit error packet. The basic idea is that the transmitter after sending the packet waits for specific time (time out) to receive an acknowledgement. If it receives positive acknowledgement (ACK), it sends the next packet. On the other hand, if it receives negative acknowledge (NAC) or timed out before receiving any acknowledgement, it then retransmits the same packet. The process repeats until an ACK has been received by the transmitter or a specific number of retransmission has been reached.

In (Tan et al., 2007), an opportunistic (hybrid implicit/explicit) acknowledgement scheme suitable for stop and wait protocols in underwater is proposed. The simple stop and wait (S &W) protocol is chosen as it is the most popular method in underwater acoustic communication due to the half-duplex property of acoustic modem. In the context of a multi hop channel, the work in (Tan et al., 2007) proposed that the acknowledgement can be achieved explicitly by transmitting an acknowledgement packet per successfully received packet, or implicitly by making use of the broadcast nature of the medium.

In (Lee et al., 2008), the channel sharing property inherent in underwater environment is utilized in proposing an efficient ARQ scheme. In this scheme packet size is controlled in such a way that transmission time becomes smaller than propagation delay. Collision free transmission between multiple nodes is achieved by scheduling packets. In a multiple hop setup, the acknowledgement packet is replaced by overhearing packet transmitted from next hop. Overhearing as an acknowledgement method not only saves energy but it also minimizes overhead and transmission latency. The scheme is evaluated by comparing it with an existing stop and wait ARQ in term of the latency, and it shows a reduction in the latency. The latency and energy efficiency is still a problem in bad channel conditions cases though.

In (Gao et al., 2009), the authors make use of the long propagation delay in underwater environment to transmit and receive in a juggling manner. This juggling scheme enables a continuous ARQ to be implemented irrespective of the half-duplex property of the acoustic modem. This scheme decreases the propagation time by having more than one packet in the channel between transmitter and receiver. This leads to high throughput compared with the other variant ARQ schemes, but it is still unsuitable in bad channel conditions or in a longer distance ranges.

In (Valera et al. 2009), a modular and lightweight of an opportunistic multi-hop ARQ (Tan et al., 2007) was implemented for real system. An extensible network stack suitable for challenged underwater acoustic networks was designed and implemented in the work. Evaluation demonstrated that the opportunistic ARQ can provide significant improvement in terms of data delivery ratio. The disadvantage of this technique is an increase in end-to-end delay due to queuing and retransmissions.

3.2 Forward error correction technique

Forward Error Correction (FEC) or error control coding is a system for achieving reliable message transmission in a communication system by correcting errors in the receiver side (hence the name 'Forward').

Recent and major activities on error control coding can be summarized as follows:

- Research on good structural properties, and high error correcting performance.
- Efficient encoding and decoding strategies.
- Applicability of coding in various transmission system and channels.

Forward error correction can be used in two levels, namely at the bit and the byte level. Bit level correction is achieved by adding redundant bits to the data in the sender. At the packet level, additional check packets are transmitted to help recover lost packets. In the FEC, no back channel is needed, but high bandwidth is required. It is therefore suitable in cases where retransmission is costly or impossible, as in broadcasting. The numbers of errors which can be corrected depend on the code rate and the type of coding used. Therefore, different FEC codes are suitable for different conditions.

There are two main types of FEC; the first one is the block codes which work on a fixed-size blocks (packets of bits or symbols), the most famous block codes are Reed-Solemn, Golay, (Bose, Chandhuri and Hocquenghem) BCH code, multidimensional parity and Hamming codes. The other type of FEC is convolutional codes, which work on bit or symbol streams of arbitrary length. It is often decoded using Viterbi algorithm, and it can be turned into block code if desired.

Most telecommunication systems use fixed types of FEC code, which is designed for the expected worst case bit error rate. These codes will fail if the bit error rate ever gets worse.

In (Guo, 2006), error recovery through network coding was explored for underwater sensor networks. The computational power of underwater sensors along with the multiple routes provided by the broadcast nature of acoustic medium are the main reasons for applying network coding. In this technique the source and intermediate nodes encode packets and send them on multiple routes. The packets are then recovered in the destination by combining packets from different routes.

In (Xie and Cui, 2007), the Segmented Data Reliable Transport protocol (SDRT) is proposed,. The protocol is a hybrid of FEC and ARQ. It sends data block by block and hop by hop. The sender encodes the packet using erasure codes, and sends it to an intermediate node. The intermediate node reconstructs the packet and encodes it and sends it to the next hop. The sender continues to send the data until it receive an acknowledgement from its next node, and this is the main problem with SDRT as it wastes energy. SDRT however improves channel utilization and simplify protocol management.

In (Liu et al., 2010; Bin et al., 2008), the Internode distance-based Redundancy Reliable Transport Protocol (ARRTP) is proposed. It is a hybrid of two types of error correction techniques which encode message on bit and/or packet level. ARRTP is based on distance as adaptation factor. For each range of distance, one or a hybrid of two techniques is used. The technique was also investigated in cooperation mode, making use of the broadcast nature of acoustic signal. ARRTP is found to have better probability of success and energy efficient in single and multi-transmission. This technique is based on fixed channel conditions analysis, so it is unsuitable in variable underwater channel conditions.

4. Transmission energy efficiency mathematical and simulation analysis

Underwater acoustic channel are characterized by variable channel conditions and variable distances between sensor nodes due to water currents. As said earlier in the chapter, in such situations, reliable and efficient communication data transport is needed. Reliability is usually achieved by using error correction techniques. However, energy consumption needs to be considered as it is difficult to recharge or even replace batteries for a large number and sparsely distributed sensors. This condition is even worse in underwater due to the harsh aquatic medium (Colin, 2007; Xie and Cui, 2007). Hence, the design of error correction techniques should take into consideration the energy conservation requirement.

In this section, we first develop a model for underwater propagation. A mathematical analysis for energy efficiency for FEC and ARQ techniques in underwater environment is then presented. The analysis is based on communication distance and packet size, and considers the effects of wind speed, and shipping factor. Simulation was done using MATLAB to validate the mathematical analysis results. Results depicting the energy efficiencies of transmission using ARQ and FEC for different packet size, different distances, and different channel conditions (wind speed and shipping factors) are presented.

4.1 Underwater propagation model

The propagation model is responsible for calculating the SNR at the receiver after attenuation and noise are taken into account. To calculate the SNR at the receiver, both the attenuation of the acoustic signal in water and the ambient noise need to be calculated. The total attenuation is calculated based on the spreading losses and Thorp approximation for the absorption loss (Urick, 1983; Yang and Liu, 2009; Liu et al., 2010; Harris and Zorzi, 2007).

4.1.1 Attenuation

Attenuation consists of two parts, the first one is the absorption loss and the second part is the spreading loss. To calculate the absorption loss at a given frequency, Thorp's approximation function divides the frequencies into two groups; one group under 400 Hz and the other one over 400 Hz as follows:

$$10\log a(f) = 0.11\frac{f^2}{1+f^2} + 44\frac{f^2}{4200+f} + 2.75\times10^{-4}f^2 + 0.003 \quad f>0.4$$

$$= 0.002 + 0.11\times(\frac{f}{1+f}) + 0.011f \quad f<0.4 \tag{1}$$

where a(f) is given in dB/km and f in KHz for underwater communications. Combining absorption effects and spreading loss, the total attenuation is as follows:

$$10\log A(l,f) = k\log l + l\times10\log a(f) \tag{2}$$

where the first term is the spreading loss and the second term is the absorption loss. The spreading coefficient k defines the geometry of the propagation (i.e., k = 1 for cylindrical propagation (shallow water), k = 2 for spherical propagation (deep water), and k = 1.5 for practical spreading) (Urick, 1983).

4.1.2 Noise

The background noise in ocean has many sources which vary with frequency and location (Wenz and Gordon, 1939). The following formulas give the power spectral density of the four noise components (Yang and Liu, 2009; Liu, 2010; Harris and Zorzi, 2007; Webb, 1992):

$$10\log N_t(f) = 17 - 30\log(f) \tag{3}$$

$$10\log N_s(f) = 40 + 20(s-0.5) + 26\log(f) - 60\log(f+0.03) \tag{4}$$

$$10\log N_w(f) = 50 + 7.5\times w^{0.5} + 20\log(f) - 40\log(f+0.4) \tag{5}$$

$$10\log N_{th}(f) = -15 + 20\log(f) \tag{6}$$

Where N_t is the noise due to turbulence, N_s is the noise due to shipping (the shipping variable s take the values between 0 and 1), N_w is the noise due to wind (the wind variables w represent wind speed in m/s), and N_{th} represents thermal noise. The overall noise power spectral density for a given frequency f (KHz) is then:

$$N(f) = N_t(f) + N_s(f) + N_w(f) + N_{th}(f) \tag{7}$$

4.1.3 Signal to noise ratio

It is well known that SNR of an emitted underwater signal at the receiver is given by (Yang and B. Liu, 2009; Harris and M. Zorzi, 2007; Brekhovskikh and Lysanov, L.1982)

$$SNR = SL - A(l,f) - N(f) - DI \tag{8}$$

where N(f), A(l,f) are in dBs given from equations (2) and (7). Assuming Omni-directional directivity, directivity index (DI) = 0. The source level $SL = 20\log I\big/1\mu Pa$, where I is the intensity at 1 m from the source in watt/m2, given by:

$$I = \frac{P_t}{2\pi H} \tag{9}$$

Where P_t is the transmission power, and H is the water depth in m.

4.2 Energy efficiency mathematical analysis

The data packet format in ARQ case can be presented as in Figure 1 (a). It consists of a header field α bits long, payload of size n bits and a Frame Check Sequence (FCS) τ bits long. The acknowledgement packet length is ack.

In FEC case it can be presented as in Figure 1 (b). It consists of a payload of size (n-k) bits long, a parity check of k bits and a header field α bits long.

Header	FCS	Payload
α	τ	n

Fig. 1. (a): ARQ Packet Format

Header	Parity check	Payload
α	k	n-k

Fig. 1. (b): FEC Packet Format

4.2.1 Optimization metric

Energy efficiency is the suitable metric which captures both energy and reliability constraints, and it is defined as (Sankarasubramaniam et al, 2003; Tian et al. , 2008):

$$\eta = \eta_e(1 - PER)$$

$$= \frac{E_{eff}}{E_{tot}}(1 - PER) \tag{10}$$

Where η is the energy efficiency, η_e is the energy throughput, r = (1-PER) is the Packet Acceptance Rate (PAR), which accounts for data reliability, and $\frac{E_{eff}}{E_{tot}}$ denotes the energy throughput. Therefore, the energy efficiency η represents the useful fraction of the total energy expenditure in a communication link between sensors.

4.2.2 Bit error rate calculation

Using 8-Phase Shift Keying (PSK) scheme as the suitable modulation techniques for underwater acoustic communication, the symbol error probability P_s for ARQ is given by (Labrador et al., 2009):

$$P_s \approx 2Q(\sqrt{2\gamma_s}\sin\frac{\pi}{M}$$ (11)

where M=8 for 8-PSK, and the bit error probability P_b is given by:

$$P_b = \frac{P_s}{3}$$ (12)

Whereas for FEC convolution code (Lee et al., 2008):

$$P_b = \frac{1}{k}\sum_{d=d_{free}}^{\infty} w(d)Q(\sqrt{2dR_c\gamma_b}$$ (13)

where w(d) is the weight distribution function, dfree is the minimum hamming distance, and γ_b is the received SNR, $R_c = \frac{k}{k+1}$ is the code rate.

4.2.3 ARQ energy efficiency mathematical analysis

Energy consumption of sensor node for communication in one hop is given by:

$$E_{ARQ} = E_{ARQ}^{tr} + E_{ARQ}^{re}$$ (14)

Where E_{ARQ}^{tr} is the energy consumed by the sender in transmitting the data and receiving the acknowledgement, and E_{ARQ}^{re} is the energy consumed by the receiver in receiving the data and transmitting the acknowledgement as presented in the following equations:

$$E_{ARQ}^{tr} = E_{data}^{tr} + E_{ack}^{re}$$

$$= P_{tr}l_{data}T_{tr} + P_{re}l_{ack}T_{tr}$$ (15)

$$E_{ARQ}^{re} = E_{data}^{re} + E_{ack}^{tr}$$

$$= P_{re}l_{data}T_{tr} + P_{tr}l_{ack}T_{tr}$$ (16)

Where $P_{tr/re}$ is the power consumed in transmitting/ receiving, and $T_{tr} = \frac{1}{R}$ is the time of transmitting 1 bit. From Figure 1 (a), using the bit error rate probability P_b in (12), and assuming independent bit errors, the Packer Error Rate (PER) for ARQ can be derived as follows:

$$PER_{ARQ} = 1 - (1 - P_b)^{n + \alpha + \tau} \tag{17}$$

This expression closely approximates PER under bursty error conditions.

From equation (9) energy efficiency of ARQ without retransmission strategy can hence be written as:

$$Eff_{ARQ} = \frac{E_{ARQ}^{eff}}{E_{ARQ}^{tot}} (1 - PER_{ARQ})$$

$$= \frac{(P_{tr} + P_{re})nT_{tr}}{(P_{tr} + P_{re})(n + \alpha + \tau + ack)T_{tr}} (1 - PER_{ARQ})$$

$$= \frac{n}{(n + \alpha + \tau + ack)} (1 - PER_{ARQ}) \tag{18}$$

where E_{ARQ}^{eff} is the energy consumed by the payload only, E_{ARQ}^{tot} is the total energy consumed.

4.2.4 FEC energy efficiency mathematical derivation

The energy consumption of FEC is given by:

$$E_{FEC} = E_{FEC}^{tr} + E_{FEC}^{re} + E_{dec} + E_{enc} \tag{19}$$

Using convolution turbo code as forward error correction techniques, encoding (Eenc) and decoding energy (Edec) are considered to be negligibly small (Sankarasubramaniam et al., 2003; Tian et al., 2008), and from Figure 1 (b), the expression for the energy efficiency is defined as:

$$Eff_{FEC} = \frac{E_{FEC}^{eff}}{E_{FEC}^{tot}} (1 - PER_{FEC})$$

$$= \frac{(P_{tr} + P_{re})(n - k)T_{tr}}{(P_{tr} + P_{re})(n + \alpha)T_{tr}} (1 - PER_{FEC})$$

$$= \frac{(n - k)}{(n + \alpha)} (1 - PER_{FEC}) \tag{20}$$

where PER_{FEC} is calculated using equation (13).

4.3 Simulation

Simulation offers a powerful tool to validate mathematical analysis. The simulation is carried out for a two system using different error correction techniques using MATLAB.

Two types of parameters are considered for design and configuration. Energy efficiency and packet probability of success (PAR) are taken as the main performance factors in comparing between the two systems.

4.3.1 Design parameters

The design parameters are the parameters that can be varied in order to study their effect on the system energy efficiency. In the first system ARQ technique is used as the error correction technique, where 8-PSK is used as the modulation technique as it is the best modulation technique in underwater channel as stated in the literature. In the second convolutional coding is used as the FEC error correction technique (Labrador et al., 2009).

The design parameters used are the distance, shipping factor and wind speed. Shipping factor and wind speed are taken as a representative for variable channel conditions; any other channel condition factor will have the same effect.

Modulation and encoding technique types and design parameters can be written as in Table 2. below:

Parameter	Description	Type or Value
Modulation	Modulation technique used in ARQ case	8-PSK
Encoding	Encoding technique used for error correction	Convolution coding
Distance	Communication distance	From 800 to 3000 m
Shipping factor	Factor describe the effect of shipping	From 0 to 1
Wind speed	Factor describe the effect of wind	Any value in m/s

Table 2. Modulation, Encoding Types and Design Parameters

4.3.2 Configuration parameters

The simulation is carried out using MATLAB.

In the transmitter a random bit generator is used with the parameters as follows:

- size of signal constellation M = 8;
- Number of bit per symbol k = 3,
- Number of bit processed n = $3e^4$.

Binary data stream are created as a column vector using the function: x = randint (n, 1);

A Bit-to-Symbol mapping which convert the bits in x into k-bit symbols is done using the following MATLAB function:

- xsym = bi2de (reshape (x, k, length (x) /k) .',' left-msb');

Then an 8-PSK modulator is used to modulate the signal with the function:

- y = modulate (modem.pskmod (M), xsys);

The value of SNR in underwater channel is calculated as in section 2.1.3., and an AWGN function is used as:

- ynoisy = awgn (y, snr, "measured');

In the receiver side 8-PSK demodulator is used to demodulate the signal using the function:

- zsym = demodulate (modem.pskdemod (M), noisy);

the Symbol-to-Bit mapping is done using the function:

- z = de2bi (zsym,'left-msb');

then BER is obtained by comparing the input x with the output z using the function:

- [number_of_errors,bit_error_rate] = biterr (x, z);

The energy efficiency is calculated from the BER as in section 2.2.3.

In the second system the 8-PSK is replaced by a convolutional encoder with the following:

Trellis is defined using the following function:

- t = poly2trellis (3, [5 7]);

Then puncturing is attained by the following function:

- punctcode = convenc (x, t, [1 1 0 1 1 0 1 0 1 0]);

This puncturing is for 5/6 code rate.

Then 0 bit is mapped to 1 and 1 bit to -1 using the function:

- tcode = 1 – 2*punctcode;

The value of SNR in underwater channel is written as in section 2.1.3., and an AWGN function is used as:

- ncode = awgn(tcode, snr, 'measured');

In the receiver side, the punctured code is decoded by viterbi using the function:

- decoded = vitdec(ncode, t, 96, 'trunc', ...'unquant', [1 1 0 1 1 0 1 0 1 0]); % Decode.

then BER is obtained by comparing the input x with the output decoded using the function:

- [numErrPE, berPE] = biterr(decoded, x);

The energy efficiency is calculated from the BER as in section 2.2.4

4.4 Results and analysis

The results are obtained using a MATLAB, assuming LinkQuest UWM2000 acoustic modem (LinQuest Inc., 2011), and the parameters as given in Table 3:

First, a suitable frequency range based on AN Factor as in Figure 2 was calculated; this frequency range corresponds to the minimum AN factor. A suitable range is found from 10 KHz up to 25 KHz, below and above this range the AN Factor increases sharply.

From Figures 3 (a) and 3 (b), it is clear that transmission energy efficiency of both techniques increases with increasing packet size in short distances, whereas decreases in long distances

Symbol	Parameters	
	Definition	Quantity
P_t	Transmitting Power	2 W
P_{re}	Receiving Power	0.75
R	Bit Data Rate	10 kbps
l_{ack}	Acknowledge packet length	7 Byte
$\alpha + \tau$	Header + FCS length	11 Byte

Table 3. Simulation Parameters

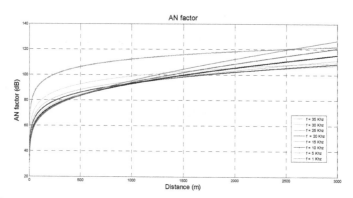

Fig. 2. AN Factor

for both techniques. It is also clear that there is only a slight differences between mathematical and simulation results which validate the results. This differences between mathematical and simulation results decreases as the number of bits transmitted in the simulation increases.

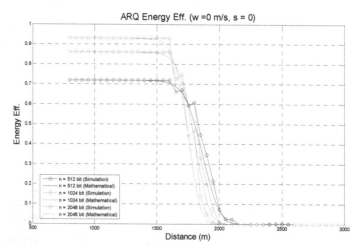

Fig. 3. (a): ARQ Transmission Energy Efficiency (Mathematical and Simulation Results)

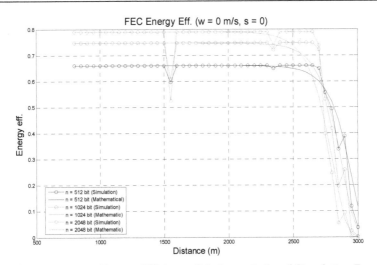

Fig. 3. (b): FEC Transmission Energy Efficiency (Mathematical and Simulation Results)

In Figure 4 (a) transmission energy efficiency of ARQ and FEC for a packet length of 512 bit is shown. It is apparent that transmission using ARQ is more energy efficient than using FEC below a specific distance (cut-off distance), and transmission using FEC is more energy efficient after this distance. The effect of shipping is unseen and can be neglected. In Figure 4 (b) the effect of wind is very clear, and the cut-off distance decreases from 1700 m when no wind exists to 1250 m when the wind speed is 1 m/s. ARQ efficiency starts to decrease at 1600 m when no wind exists, and at 1100 m when the wind speed is 1 m/s, whereas for FEC it starts to decrease at 2500 m when no wind exist and at 1800 m when the wind speed is 1 m/s.

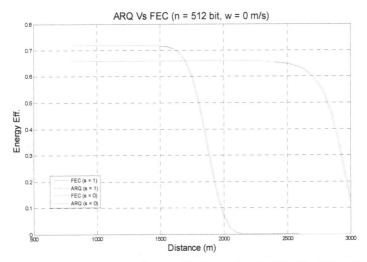

Fig. 4. (a): ARQ Vs FEC Transmission Energy Efficiency (n = 512 bit, Variable Shipping Factor)

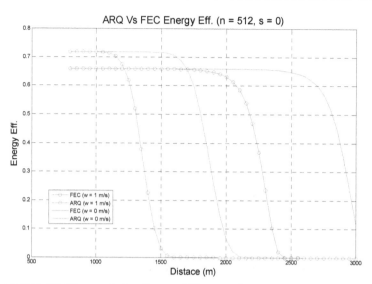

Fig. 4. (b): ARQ Vs FEC Transmission Energy Efficiency (n = 512 bit, Variable Wind Speed)

4.5 Discussion

A mathematical analysis for the energy efficiencies of ARQ and FEC data transmission has been presented. Simulation results validate the mathematical derivation results. It is found that transmission energy efficiency in underwater environment increases with increasing packet size in short distances and decreases with packet size in longer distances. It is also found that transmission using ARQ is more energy efficient below a specific distance (cut-off distance), whereas transmission using FEC is more efficient after that distance. This cut-off distance is affected by wind speed. Shipping factor has been found to have no effect on this frequency values. From those results we can say that variable distances and variable channel conditions which characterize underwater channel make it energy inefficient to use one or fixed type of error correction techniques in transmission.

The results obtained from this part will be the basis for designing and implementing a new adaptive hybrid energy efficient error correction protocol for underwater wireless sensor networks in the next part.

5. Adaptive hybrid energy efficient error correction technique for UWSN

As it is energy inefficient in transmission to use one or fixed type of error correction in realistic underwater conditions, it is important to consider hybrid error correction technique. This hybrid error correction technique must adapt to the variation in channel conditions and to the variation in distances between sensor nodes.

In this section, we propose an Adaptive Hybrid Energy Efficient Error Correction (AHEC) technique for Underwater Wireless Sensor Networks (UWSN) data transmission. The proposed technique depends on an adaptation algorithm which determines the most energy efficient error correction technique for the current channel conditions and distance. The adaptation algorithm is based on the current Bit Error Rate (BER), current error correction technique, and a pre-calculated Packet Acceptance Rate (PAR) ranges look-up table which is pre-calculated using the energy efficiency derivation has been done in the previous section. Based on this, a periodical 3-bit feedback is added to the acknowledgement packet to tell the sender which error correction technique is most suitable for current channel conditions and distance. The error correction is chosen from a pure ARQ in a good channel conditions and short distances to a hybrid of ARQ and FEC with variable encoding rates in bad channel condition and over longer distance ranges.

This section is organized as follows: the in adaptive hybrid error correction technique is presented in section 5.1. In section 5.2 we show how the pre-calculated PAR ranges look-up table is calculated. Then in section 5.3, we compare the proposed AHEC technique with the techniques that use only ARQ or only FEC as the error correction technique in variable channel conditions and over variable distance ranges.

5.1 Adaptive hybrid error correction technique main concepts

The results of the derivations in the previous section state that transmission energy efficiency varies with the variation in transmission distances and channel conditions for both the ARQ and the FEC. Depending on the underwater network condition and the internode distances, one technique will be better than the other. The propose AHEC technique is designed to achieve high transmission energy efficiency in such conditions, by adaptively changing the error correction technique used.

The technique works like this: for variable distances and variable channel conditions, AHEC technique always search for the technique with the highest energy efficiency, and since reliability is one part in transmission energy efficiency calculation as stated in equation (10), it will also be a reliable technique. The technique depends on an adaptation algorithm which based on the current PAR, current encoding technique used, and a pre-calculated PAR ranges look-up table to determine which error correction technique is most suitable for the current distance and current channel conditions. AHEC technique can designed as in the diagram Figure 5.

In AHEC technique, only modulation technique (i.e. ARQ) is used in good channel conditions and short distances, which means low BER. In bad channel conditions and long distances a hybrid of ARQ and variable code rates convolutional encoding are used.

Variable code rates are obtained using puncturing technique by deleting a part of the bits of low-rate convolution code (Begin et al., 1990), as in Table 4., and it is represented in

Code rate	Puncturing Matrix
2/3	[1 1 0 1]
3/4	[1 1 0 1 1 0]
4/5	[1 1 0 1 1 0 1 0]
5/6	[1 1 0 1 1 0 1 0 1 0]
6/7	[1 1 0 1 1 0 1 0 1 0 1 0]

Table 4. Puncturing Matrix

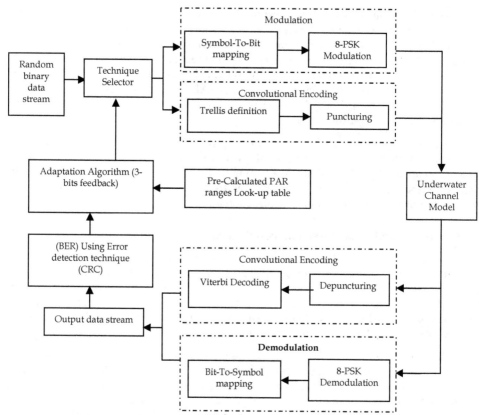

Fig. 5. AHEC Technique Design

MATLAB using systematic puncturing convolution codes with the parameters obtained from (Begin et al., 1990) as shown in Table 5.

R_c	2/3	3/4	4/5	5/6	6/7
d_{free}	3	3	2	2	2
W_{dfree}	1	15	1	2	5
$W_{dfree+1}$	10	104	36	111	186
$W_{dfree+2}$	54	540	309	974	1942
$W_{dfree+3}$	226	2520	2058	6815	16428
$W_{dfree+4}$	853	11048	12031	43598	124469
$W_{dfree+5}$	3038	46516	65754	263671	887512
$W_{dfree+6}$	10432	190448	344656	1536563	6088910
$W_{dfree+7}$	34836	763944	1755310	8724988	40664781
$W_{dfree+8}$	114197	3016844	8754128	46801477	266250132

Table 5. Minimum Hamming Distances (dfree) and Weight Distribution (wdfree) for Variable Rate Convolutional Codes.

5.1.1 AHEC technique adaptation algorithm

The adaptation algorithm is as follows:

Using error detection technique in the receiver, BER is periodically calculated, and from the BER, PAR is calculated using the packet length n as:

$$PAR = (1 - BER)^n \qquad (21)$$

Then the suitable error correction technique is calculated from the function:

$$J = f(PAR, I, PARMAX(I, J), PARMIN(I, J)) \qquad (22)$$

where J is the suitable error correction technique required, PAR is the current packet acceptance rate, I is the current error correction technique used, and PARMAX(I,J), PARMIN(I,J) are the pre-calculated PAR ranges look-up.

We can mathematically model this function as in the following formula:

$$J = \sum_{n=1}^{6} n \times I_{A_i^n}(PAR) \qquad (23)$$

where A_i^n is a look-up table taken from the energy efficiency derivation of six error correction techniques (One ARQ and five varying code rates FEC), and

$$I_B(x) = \begin{cases} 1....if.x \in B \\ 0.....otherwise \end{cases} \qquad (24)$$

From the value of J obtained, a 3-bit feedback is added to the acknowledgement to state which error correction technique to use as in Table 6. below:

Correction Technique	Consists of	FEC Code Rate	Feedback
1	Pure ARQ		000
2	Hybrid ARQ& FEC	6/7	001
3	Hybrid ARQ& FEC	5/6	010
4	Hybrid ARQ& FEC	4/5	011
5	Hybrid ARQ& FEC	3/4	100
6	Hybrid ARQ& FEC	2/3	101

Table 6. Error Correction Techniques Details

5.2 Pre-calculated PAR ranges look-up table calculations

The pre-calculated PAR ranges look-up table is calculated as follows:

1. Transmission energy efficiencies and PARs using six error correction techniques (One ARQ plus five variable code rates FECs) for variable values of SNR are found as in section 2.2.3 and section 2.2.4.

2. Starting with the SNR values which gives PAR values equal to 1 for all the techniques; at this SNR ARQ will have the maximum energy efficiency compared to the others, so the PAR for all those technique at this point is the maximum values in the ranges which makes the suitable technique is technique 1 (pure ARQ). This means $PARMAX_{J,1} = 1$, i.e. if the current technique is J and the current PAR is in the range that has 1 as the maximum value, then technique one is the most energy efficient technique.

3. Then decreasing SNR value until the energy efficiency of the first technique is less than the energy efficiency of the second technique; at this SNR the PAR for all technique will be the minimum values in the ranges which makes the suitable technique is technique 1 (pure ARQ). This means the PAR of any technique J at this point = $PARMIN_{J,1}$, i.e. if the PAR of the current technique J is in between $PARMIN_{J,1}$ and $PARMAX_{J1}$, then technique one is the most energy efficient technique. As the minimum values in the first ranges equal the maximum values in the second range, then:

$$PARMAX_{J,2} = PARMIN_{J,1}$$

Then decreasing SNR value until the energy efficiency of the second technique is less than the energy efficiency of the third technique; at this SNR the PAR for all technique will be the minimum values in the ranges which makes the suitable technique is technique number two.

This means the PAR of any technique J at this point = $PARMIN_{J,2}$ i.e. if the PAR of the current technique J is in between $PARMIN_{J,2}$ and $PARMAX_{J,2}$, then technique number 2 is the most energy efficient technique.

As the minimum values in the second ranges equal the maximum values in the third range, then:

$$PARMAX_{J,3} = PARMIN_{J,2}$$

4. Then decreasing SNR value until the energy efficiency of the third technique is less than the energy efficiency of the fourth technique; at this SNR the PAR for all technique will be the minimum values in the ranges which makes the suitable technique is technique number 3.

This means the PAR of any technique J at this point = $PARMIN_{J,3}$ i.e. if the PAR of the current technique J is in between $PARMIN_{J,3}$ and $PARMAX_{J,3}$, then technique number 3 is the most energy efficient technique.

As the minimum values in the third ranges equal the maximum values in the fourth range, then:

$$PARMAX_{J,4} = PARMIN_{J,3}$$

5. Then decreasing SNR value until the energy efficiency of the fourth technique is less than the energy efficiency of the fifth technique; at this SNR the PAR for all technique

will be the minimum values in the ranges which makes the suitable technique is technique number 4.

This means the PAR of any technique J at this point = $PARMIN_{J,4}$ i.e. if the PAR of the current technique J is in between $PARMIN_{J,4}$ and $PARMAX_{J,4}$, then technique number 4 is the most energy efficient technique.

As the minimum values in the fourth ranges equal the maximum values in the fifth range, then:

$$PARMAX_{J,5} = PARMIN_{J,4}$$

6. Then decreasing SNR value until the energy efficiency of the fifth technique is less than the energy efficiency of the six technique; at this SNR the PAR for all technique will be the minimum values in the ranges which makes the suitable technique is technique 5.

    This means the PAR of any technique J at this point = $PARMIN_{J,5}$ i.e. if the PAR of the current technique J is in between $PARMIN_{J,5}$ and $PARMAX_{J,5}$, then technique number 5 is the most energy efficient technique.

    As the minimum values in the fifth ranges equal the maximum values in the sixth range, then:

$$PARMAX_{J,6} = PARMIN_{J,5}$$

7. At last zero will be the minimum values for the ranges that makes technique six is the most energy efficient technique ($PARMIN_{J,6} = 0$, for all techniques).

5.3 Results and discussion

In this section we first present how to calculate the pre-calculated PAR ranges look-up table, which is an essential part in our adaptation algorithm, then we will compare our AHEC technique with the previous works in the literature that depend on only ARQ or only FEC for error correction (Lee et al., 2008; Gao et al., 2009; Tan et al., 2003; Xie and Cui, 2007) in variable channel conditions and variable distances.

5.3.1 AHEC technique transmission energy efficiency calculations

To calculate the pre-calculated PAR ranges look-up table, energy efficiencies versus PARs for the six techniques are calculated as in section 2.2.3 for ARQ and in section 2.2.4 for the five variable code rate FEC, then the pre-calculated PAR ranges look-up table can be calculated as in section 3.3, and it can be displayed as in Table 7 below:

i\j	1	2	3	4	5	6
1	0.95 -1.0	0.95 – 0.0				
2	1.0	0.89 – 1.0	0.84 -0.89	0.62-0.84	0.32-0.62	0. 00-0.32
3	1.0	0.92 -1.0	0.89 -0.92	0.72 -0.89	0.45-0.72	0.00-0.45
4	1.0	0.96 -1.0	0.94 -0.96	0.85 – 0.94	0.68 -.85	0.00 – 0.68
5	1.0	0.98 – 1.0	0.97 – 0.98	0.92- 0.97	0.81–0.92	0.00 -0.81
6	1.0	0.995 – 1.0	0.992 -0.995	0.992 -0.98	0.95 – 0.98	0.00 – 0.95

Table 7. Pre-Calculated Look-Up PAR Ranges Table

From the Pre-calculated PAR ranges look-up table above, and from the current PAR, current encoding technique, AHECT energy efficiency can be calculated as in section 3.2

5.3.2 Transmission using AHEC technique versus the transmission using ARQ and FEC transmission energy efficiency

Figure 6 below gives a comparison between the energy efficiency of transmission using AHEC technique and the transmission using pure ARQ and pure FEC for varying distances.

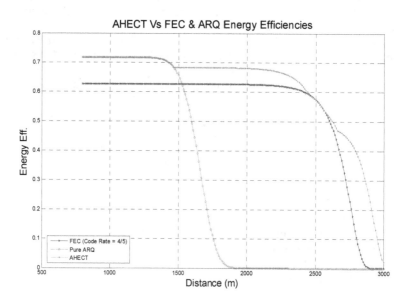

Fig. 6. AHEC Technique Vs ARQ & FEC Energy Efficiency (Variable Distances Case)

From this figure it is clear that transmission using AHEC technique is more energy efficient than using both ARQ and FEC in variable distances situation.

Compared with the pure ARQ, transmission using AHEC technique achieves 10 % increase in saving energy when the distance is around 1500 m and more than 60 % when the distance increases above 1700 m. When compared with transmission using FEC, it achieves around 10 % increase in energy saving when the distance is below 1500 m, and around 7 % saving when the distance goes above 1500 m.

In Figure 7; variable wind speed is taken as a measure for the variation in channel conditions. From this Figure it is clear that transmission using AHEC technique is more energy efficient than both techniques using ARQ and FEC for variable wind speed (i.e. variable channel conditions). Compared with the pure ARQ, and when the transmission distance is 1500 m, transmission using AHEC technique achieves 6 % increase in energy saving when wind speed is 0.5 m/s, more than 50 % energy saving when wind speed

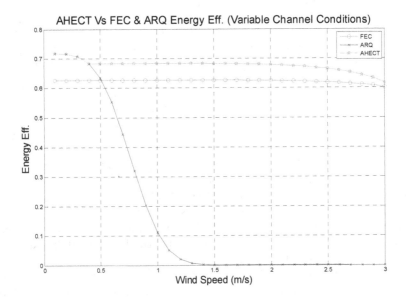

Fig. 7. AHEC Technique Vs ARQ & FEC Transmission Energy Efficiency (Variable Channel Conditions)

increases to 1 m/s, and more than 60 % when wind speed is greater than 1.5 m/s. When compared with transmission using FEC, transmission using AHEC technique achieves around 8 % increase in energy saving when wind speed is below 0.5 m/s and around 6 % when wind speed is more than 0.5 m/s.

6. Conclusions

Underwater wireless sensor network (UWSN) is a promising engineering endeavour which will ensure progress in monitoring and exploiting the ocean's vast resources. But until now it faces many challenges, the most important of which is the severe energy constraint of the batteries, which cannot be recharged or replaced in aquatic medium. Complicating the issue is the variability of the channel conditions and the distances between underwater sensors.

In this chapter, we have mathematically analyzed the transmission energy efficiency for two main error correction techniques, ARQ and FEC, in underwater environment. A simulation is done to validate the mathematical derivation results. Transmission using ARQ is found to be more energy efficient than transmission using FEC below specific distances, and transmission using FEC is found to be better after that. We call this specific distance the cut-off distance. We found that this cut-off distance is not fixed and varies with the variation in channel conditions and packet size.

Based on the mathematical analysis, we have proposed an energy efficient Adaptive Hybrid Error Correction (AHEC) technique for transmission. The proposed technique adaptively changes the error correction technique to the technique with the highest transmission energy efficiency compared to the others. An adaptation algorithm which based on the current packet acceptance rate (PAR), current encoding technique, and a pre-calculated PAR ranges look-up table has been proposed. From the output of the adaptation algorithm, a periodic 3-bit feedback is sent to the sender indicating which error correction technique is most suitable given the current distance and channel conditions. The proposed technique has been compared with techniques that use only ARQ or FEC. The results show that our proposed technique is more energy efficient than either of them.

7. References

Akyildiz, I. Pompili, D. and Melodia, T. (2004). Challenges for Efficient Communication in Underwater Acoustic Sensor Networks, *ACM Sigbed Review*, Vol. 1, 2004.

Akyildiz, I. Pompili, D. and Melodia, T. (2005). Underwater acoustic sensor networks: research challenge, Ad Hoc Networks (Elsevier), Vol. 3, pp. (257-279), 2005.

Begin, G. Haccoun, D. and Paquin, C. (1990). Further Results on High - Rate Puncturing G Convolutional codes for viterbi and sequential decoding, IEEE transaction on Communications, Vol. 38, pp. (1922-1928), 1990.

Bin, L. Garcin, F. Ren, F. and Lin, C. (2008). A study of forward error correction schemes for reliable transport in underwater sensor networks, Proceedings of the 5th Annual IEEE Communications Society Conference on Sensor, Mesh and Ad Hoc Communications and Networks (SECON '08), pp (197–205), 2008.

Brekhovskikh, L. and Lysanov, Y. (2003). Fundamental of ocean acoustics: Springer, 1982.

Colin Y., Chan, and Motani M. (2007). An integrated energy efficient data retrieval protocol for underwater delay tolerant networks, Proceeding of IEEE ocean'07, Aberdeen, Scotland, 2007.

Gao, M. Soh, W. and Tao, M. (2009). A transmission scheme for continuous ARQ protocols over underwater acoustic channels, Proceeding of the 2009 IEEE international conference on Communications (ICC'09), 2009.

Guo, Z. Xie, P. Cui, J. and Wang, B. (2006). On applying network coding to underwater sensor networks, Proceedings of ACM WUWNet'06, Los Angeles, CA, 2006.

Harris, A. and Zorzi, M. (2007). Modelling the underwater acoustic channel in ns2, Proceedings of the 2nd international conference on Performance evaluation methodologies and tools, 2007.

Joshy, S. and Babu, A. (2010). Capacity of Underwater Wireless Communication Channel with Different Acoustic Propoagation Loss Models, *International Journal of Computer Networks & Communications (IJCNC)*, Vol. 2, 2010.

Kunal K., Tripathi R. and Singh V. (2010). An HARQ based Optimized Error Correction Technique, International Journal of Computer Applications, Vol. 9, 2010.

Labrador, Y. Karimi, M. Pan, D. And Miller, J. (2009). Modulation and error correction in the underwater acoustic communication channel, International Journal of Computer Science and Network Security, Vol. 9, pp. (123-130), 2009.

Lee J. Kim J. Lee J. Jang Y. and Dho K. (2008). An improved ARQ scheme in underwater acoustic sensor networks, Proc. MTS/IEEE Oceans, Kobe, Japan, 2008, pp. 1-5.

Lee, W. Kim, J. Lee, J. Jang, Y and Dho, K. (2008). An improved ARQ scheme in underwater acoustic sensor networks, Proceeding of MTS/IEEE Oceans, Kobe, Japan, pp. (1-5), 2008.

LinkQuest Inc. Underwater Acoustic Modem Models. June 2010 (Available: http://www.link-quest.com)

Liu, B. Chen, H. Lei, X. Ren, F. and Sezaki, K. (2010). Internode distance-based redundancy reliable transport in underwater sensor networks, EURASIP J. Wireless Comm. and Networking, 2010.

Lin S., Costello D., Miller M., (1984) Automatic-Repeat-Request Error-Control Schemes. IEEE Communications Magazine. pp (5-17), 1984.

Pompili, D. (2007). *Efficient communication protocols for underwater acoustic sensor networks,"* PhD, School of Electrical and Computer Engineering, Georgia Institute of Technology, 2007.

Preisig, J. (2007). Acoustic Propagation considerations for underwater Acoustic communications network Development , SIGMOBILE Mob. Computer Commun. Rev., Vol. 11, pp. (2-10), 2007.

S. Joshy and A. Babu, "Capacity of Underwater Wireless Communication Channel with Different Acoustic Propoagation Loss Models," International Journal of Computer Networks & Communications (IJCNC), vol. 2, 2010.

Sankarasubramaniam, Y. Akyidiliz, I. and Mclaughlin, S. (2003). Energy efficiency based packet size optimization in wireless sensor networks , Proceeding of the 1st IEEE International Workshop on Sensor Network Protocols and Applications SNPA'03 (held in conjunction with IEEE ICC'03), Anchorage, Alaska, USA, 2003.

Stojanovic, M. and Preisig. J. (2009). Underwater Acoustic Communication Channels: Propagation Models and Statistical Characterization, IEEE Communications, pp. 84-89, 2009.

Tan H., Seah W. and Doyle L. (2007). A multi-hop ARQ protocol for underwater acoustic networks, Proceedings of OCEANS 2007 , Europe, 18-21 June 2007 pp. 1 - 6.

Tian, Z. Yan, D. and Liang, Q. (2008). Energy efficiency analysis of error control schemes in wireless sensor networks, Proceeding of International Wireless Communications and Mobile Computing Conference, IWCMC '08, pp. (401-405), 2008.

Urick R. J. (1983). Principles of Underwater Sound, McGraw-Hill, New York.

Valera, A. Lee, P. Tan, H. (2009). Implementation and Evaluation of Multihop ARQ for Reliable Communications in Underwater Acoustic Networks, Proceedings of the IEEE OCEANS Conference, Bremen, Germany, 2009.

Webb, S. (1992). The equilibrium oceanic microseism spectrum, J. Acoust. Soc., Vol. 92, pp. (2141-2158), 1992.

Wenz and Gordon, M. (1936). Acoustic Ambient Noise in the Ocean: Spectra and Sources, The Journal of the Acoustical Society of America, Vol. 34, 1936.

Xie P. (2007). Underwater acoustic sensor networks: Medium access control, routing and reliable transfer, 2007.

Xie, P. and Cui, J. (2007). An FEC- based reliable data transport protocol for Underwater sensor networks, Proc. of 16th International Conference on Computer Communications and Networks, pp.(747-753), 2007.

Yang H. and Liu B. (2009). Optimization of Energy Efficient Transmission in Underwater Sensor Networks, Proceedings of CoRR, 2009.

2

Achieving Energy Efficiency in Analogue and Mixed Signal Integrated Circuit Design

E. López-Morillo, F. Márquez,
T. Sánchez-Rodríguez, C.I. Luján-Martínez and F. Munoz
Electronics Engineering Department, Universidad de Sevilla
Spain

1. Introduction

Wireless communications are one of the major successes of the engineering over the past two decades. The progress made in this area has not only produced a huge technological growth, but also a great impact at social and economical level. In fact, the possibility of being connected anywhere at any time has radically changed people habits.

The evolution of wireless communications is obviously linked to the power consumption of devices, which also continues increasing due to the growing amount of data and transmission speed required by the new communication standards. In contrast, the energy available in portable batteries does not grow at the same rate, improving only their capacity in a 10% every two years (Shahab, 2010). This leads to an increasingly gap between power needs and battery capacity. Therefore, energy efficiency of electronics systems has become a crucial factor to maximize the lifetime of the available batteries and one of the most important research topics in integrated circuits design in recent years.

The increase in power consumption is less dramatic for the digital domain, since it is partially compensated, as the technology scales-down, by the reduction of the supply voltage and the geometrical dimensions of a single device. The main reason for decreasing the supply voltage in modern CMOS technology is to avoid the possible breakdown of the transistors due to the extremely thin oxide. For a CMOS logic gate, e.g. an inverter, the simplest logic cell, the power consumption can be expressed as:

$$P = C_L \cdot V_{dd}^2 \cdot f \qquad (1)$$

where C_L is the load capacitor at the output of the inverter, V_{dd} is the supply voltage and f is the operating frequency. Despite of the ever-increasing working speed, the power consumption in CMOS logic circuits is reduced as the supply voltage and geometry sizes scale down. For instance, the power consumption of microprocessors is reduced in a 50% for each technology generation if the supply voltage scales down in a 30% (Bokar, 1999) and according to Gene's law, the power dissipation in embedded DSP processors will be decreased by a half every 18 months. As it will be explained later, this relative "low cost" of digital computation in terms of power dissipation, supports the idea of maximizing the digitization level of an electronic system not only to dismiss the fabrication costs but also as a way of reducing its power consumption.

The System-On-Chip (SoC) trend is the main cause for the analogue and mixed-signal and digital integrated circuits (ICs) to be fabricated on the same wafer. This fact eventually requires the analogue and mixed-signal ICs to be fabricated in modern CMOS technologies to save cost. However, several challenges are encountered in the scaling-down of the CMOS technologies for analogue designs with not much clear advantages (Yao et al. 2006). The threshold voltage is not scaled as aggressively as the supply voltage to avoid leakage current in transistors. As a consequence, the available signal swing is lower and a reduction of the noise of the circuit to maintain the same dynamic range is required. Reducing thermal noise increases the power consumption of analogue and mixed-signal circuitry. Particularly, in discrete time applications, reducing circuit noise means increasing the capacitances which results in higher power consumption in order to maintain the same operation speed. Additionally, as technologies are scaled down, the output resistance of the MOS transistors decreases resulting in lower op-amp gain. In order to increase the gain, it is required to use either cascode transistors or cascade amplifiers, increasing the complexity of the circuits. These solutions worsen the swing problems and increase the power consumption.

The analogue-to-digital (A/D) converter is one of the most important and power consuming building blocks in modern electronics systems. Moreover, A/D converter (ADC) requirements tend to be more stringent as the analogue functionality is moved to the digital domain. In recent years, the demand of more and more performance (speed and/or resolution) within a limited energy budget has pushed the IC research community to put a huge effort into increasing the energy efficiency of the ADCs. For instance, data collected from the literature over the last years indicate that the power efficiency of ADCs has improved by a factor of two every two years (Murmann, 2008), allowing some designs to become portable, such as those for biomedical applications. Due to this fact, a special attention to ADC architectures will be taken in some sections of this chapter, as they are the most limiting blocks in recent systems.

In portable bio-signals acquisition micro-systems, the power consumption requirements are taken to the extreme. For instance, medical implant devices, such as modern pacemakers, require extremely low power consumption (about 10-40 µW) in order to operate up to 10 years or more using a small non-rechargeable battery (Yeknami et al., 2010).

In wearable electronics for biomedical monitoring applications, extreme miniaturization is required and this will limit the battery size and power draw. Wearable electroencephalography (EEG) is a good example of such a power-limited system. EEG records the voltage between electrodes placed on the scalp and provides a non-invasive interface to the brain. Discrete, lightweight and comfortable devices are essential for user acceptance in applications such as epilepsy diagnosis (Casson & Rodriguez-Villegas, 2011). Long-term EEG monitoring of patients in their daily environment is generally required for epilepsy diagnosis. As these types of medical tests can take long periods of time, ultra-low power and miniaturized electronics systems need to be developed.

Another interesting arising application is the Energy Autonomous Sensors (EAS) which will represent a revolution in the use of wireless technologies, such as wireless sensor networks, in the ambient intelligence paradigms. Exploiting this continuously improving energy efficiency and advances in energy harvesting, miniaturized battery-less sensors that do not need to be recharged for their whole operational life are becoming possible nowadays (Belleville et al. 2010).

In the second section of the chapter, we give a summary on the most common techniques that have been used by the IC research community in the last years to reduce the power consumption in analogue and mixed signal circuits. Several references to relevant works where each technique is detailed are provided. The following four general categories have been considered to classify the presented techniques:

- Biasing point optimization.
- Digitally assisted techniques.
- Analogue circuitry simplification.
- Efficient use of biasing.

The authors' main contribution in this chapter is described in the third section. Some of the techniques commented on section two will be illustrated with some actual designs, a micropower channel filter for an Ultra Low Power Bluetooth (ULPBT) receiver and a compact continuous time (CT) Sigma Delta ($\Sigma\Delta$) modulator for a sensor interface powered by a passive Radio Frequency Identification (RFID) front-end.

2. Power reduction techniques in analogue integrated circuit design

2.1 Biasing point optimization

CMOS technology is used in most of the electronic devices because of its high density of integration. Traditional analysis of MOS circuits is often based on the assumption that every transistor is operating in the strong inversion region, although signal amplification can be done in any of the three inversion regions. The better knowledge of the strong inversion models and equations is one of the main reasons for its use.

Although simple MOS amplifier stages have much higher bandwidths in the strong inversion region, parameters like voltage gain, power dissipation, white noise, and distortion can be optimized by operating in the weak or moderate inversion regions (Binkley et al., 2003; D. J. Comer & D. T. Comer, 2004a, 2004b; Vittoz, 1994). Most often operation in weak inversion is synonymous to minimum power operation (Markovic et al., 2010).

There are several advantages that make operating in weak inversion an interesting issue:

1. It is possible to achieve higher gains (Allen & Holberg, 2002; D. J. Comer & D. T. Comer, 2004; Gray et al., 2001; Tsividis, 2002).
2. Low power consumption can be achieved as the quiescent drain current needed for this level of inversion is quite low.
3. Lower distortion compared to the strong inversion region (D. J. Comer & D. T. Comer, 2004a, 2004b).
4. Higher output resistance of the devices of the input stage due to the low drain currents of transistors operating in weak inversion region.

But there are also some disadvantages when designing in weak inversion region. The most important is the reduction in circuit bandwidth and therefore in frequency operation, although, they can be maximized if some issues are taken into account. In a single transistor, the maximum operating frequency is determined by the gate capacitances, C_{GS} and C_{GD}. In order to maximize the device bandwidth, these capacitors need to be kept as small as possible which is achieved with minimum transistor width and length.

In order to improve MOS modelling techniques, a large amount of research has been done until this moment regarding transistor MOS operation at the three levels of inversion (Binkley et al., 2003; Vittoz, 2009). All this research has been quite useful to define accurate equations for the weak inversion region, as for instance the EKV model (Enz et al., 1995).

Many analogue circuits have been designed using weak inversion region, such as operational transconductance amplifiers (Chanapromma et al., 2010), filters (Corbishley& Rodríguez-Villegas, 2007; Omeni, 2005), ADCs (Farshidi&Alaei-sheini, 2009; Ou et al., 2006), etc., all of them performing very low power consumption.

2.2 Digitally assisted techniques

Recent CMOS technologies open an interesting possibility for ADC design by translating analogue precision problems to the digital domain, where higher frequency signals can be processed at much lower energy cost. The additional complexity of digital processing circuits can be compensated by relaxing the analogue requirements and, as a consequence, lowering the total required energy per conversion.

Digitally assisted techniques have become a major concern in ADC design nowadays. Some traditional A/D conversion architectures (such as Successive-Approximation-Register-based -SAR- and $\Sigma\Delta$ ADCs) can be considered digitally assisted architectures since they make extensive use of CMOS digital logic. On the one hand, oversampling is a widely implemented technique in $\Sigma\Delta$ converters with high energy efficiency. As modern technologies allow a more efficient digital data processing, there are trends to extend these techniques to other Nyquist ADC architectures to decrease the required energy per conversion. On the other hand, there are a great number of approaches based on compensating errors generated in the analogue parts (such as mismatch and offset of the comparators) by means of implementing redundancy-based architectures and digital calibration methods instead of very power-demanding analogue compensation techniques.

In next sections, some of the most interesting trends involving digitally assisted techniques will be explained.

2.2.1 Digital calibration and redundancy

As it was commented before, the analogue circuits suffer some difficulties due to the MOSFET size reduction. One of the most applied techniques to compensate these errors is to introduce some digital calibration schemes, usually employing redundancy-based ADC architectures.

As an example, a widely employed architecture in wireless communication systems to reach fast operation at very high frequencies is the Flash ADC. Traditionally, these schemes have been characterized by using very power-demanding topologies with multiple gain stages for offset compensation. Actually, there are different design trends, mainly based on "relaxed precision" comparators redundancy combined with digital error compensation of mismatch and offset deviations. A first approach is illustrated in (Flynn et al., 2003), where a bank of comparators with a factor-four redundancy is implemented with no special care about their offset or mismatch properties, drastically decreasing the consumption in the analogue blocks. In an initial calibration phase, the most suitable comparator for every input range is selected and the rest are powered down, with no contribution to power consumption of the system. Another example is a Flash ADC using process variations to generate the input references from random comparators offsets (Sundström & Alvandpour, 2009), whose resolution and input signal range are optimized by means of digital calibration.

A great variety of similar approaches combining redundancy and digital error correction methods can be implemented in a similar way. For instance, there are redundancy-based ADC with a current trimming DAC for error compensation to minimize the input-referred offset of the comparators (Park et al., 2007) or partially redundant schemes -with only some additional comparators- with background calibration implemented during conversion, as shown in (Kijima et al., 2009).

2.2.2 Time-Interleaving

Time-Interleaving (TI) technique is a method based on the concept of running a system with M parallel channels by taking just one sample alternatively from each one. As a consequence, the ADC as a block would operate at an M times higher frequency than each individual channel. This allows reaching higher operation frequencies at no additional cost of analogue power consumption. However, mismatch between channels (usually the most limiting factors are offset and gain mismatch and clock skew errors) will reduce the resolution of the system. It is possible to compensate these errors using digital calibration or post processing.

An example of this technique can be found on (Cao et al., 2009), where a 6-bit Time-interleaving ADC working at 1.25 GS/s without any off-line calibration, error correction or post processing has been designed. The proposed architecture has been implemented using a two time-interleaved SAR ADCs topology combined with flash ADC sub-conversion processes, allowing a reduction from 65 to 6 comparators and lowering its power consumption well below typical values for state-of-art flash ADCs without digital calibration techniques. Another example of a Time-interleaving 7-bit SAR ADC working at 2.5 GHz is described on (Alpman et al., 2009). The proposed scheme is based on 16 parallel ADC running at 1.25GS/s with two additional ADC to allow background calibration to compensate offset and mismatch errors. Timing calibration can be done by means of adjusting a programmable delay line, which can be done during the packet header of the communication standard used for data transmission.

2.2.3 Time-domain processing

With the evolution of CMOS fabrication processes, higher bandwidth is available for analogue designers. Therefore, systems that process signals in the time domain can benefit of the improved speeds to achieve larger resolutions. Traditional time-based architectures, such as dual-slope converters, can achieve very high resolution at the cost of large conversion times. Nowadays, as technology scales down, such time-based architectures are not only limited to low speed applications.

A good example of achieving high-energy efficiency using time-domain processing and an extensive use of digital logic is the ADC architecture presented in (Yang & Sharpeshkar, 2005, 2006). They propose a current-mode ADC that works like a pipelined converter which performs the residue amplification and subtraction in time domain, without the use of conventional amplifiers. The ADC is made of only two matched capacitors, a comparator and a switched reference current source controlled by a digital state machine. Since only a single comparator and one reference current source are used for the entire conversion process, the ADC consumes minimal power and avoids inaccuracies due to gain errors and offsets.

In (Jimenez-Irastorza et al. 2011) an interesting Time-to-Digital converter (TDC) achieving high energy efficiency is presented. It implements a recursive successive approximation algorithm in the time domain to perform the conversion with a low-voltage fully digital circuitry and very low power consumption.

Another example of a simplified scheme lowering power consumption in a $\Sigma\Delta$ ADC is presented in (Colodro & Torralba, 2008). This paper presents a CT $\Sigma\Delta$ modulator where the N-bit Flash quantizer is replaced by an asynchronous comparator. As a result, the feedback signal is coded in the time-domain as a PWM signal.

2.3 Analogue circuitry simplification

In previous sections, the way of successfully translating most of the analogue complexity to the digital domain by applying some techniques has been discussed. Another complementary approach to improve power efficiency could be based on the design of simplified analogue sub-circuits, allowing higher speed operation and power consumption decrease in basic building blocks. These techniques would include not only system level designs strategies but also analogue basic topologies that can be applied to many different architectures. In this way, higher energy efficiency can be obtained also at SoC level.

In the next sections, a review of some of the most interesting approaches for circuitry simplification will be provided.

2.3.1 Switched Op-amp and Op-amp sharing

Op-amps are usually one the most power-consuming basic analogue blocks; therefore, a feasible option to reduce power consumption is to minimize their number in designs. Many switched-capacitor circuits need an active op-amp only during one clock phase, the amplification phase. As a consequence, there are two widely used techniques to reduce the number of active op-amps (Kim et al, 2006); one shares op-amps between successive stages and the other switches them off during the sampling phase.

Op-amp sharing is a technique based on using the op-amp for two adjacent stages in successive alternative phases. This technique is widely implemented in pipelined ADCs (Hashemi & Shoaei, 2007; Sasidhar, 2009), but can be applied to any op-amp based topology.

Two-stage Class-A switched-op-amp (SO) is the most popular solution for low power switched capacitor (SC) sigma-delta modulators with ultra low supply voltage conditions. The SO saves about 30%-40% of the total power since its output stage is just turned off at the integrating phase. For instance, an application to implement a 4th order band-pass $\Sigma\Delta$

modulator using switched op-amps is presented in (Kuo & Liu, 2004). While a classic op-amp topology would require four integrators working in two phases, in the proposed architecture the $\Sigma\Delta$ modulator is implemented only with two switched op-amps, drastically reducing the power consumption. To further increase efficiency, class AB output and input stages can be used in the op-amp implementation. In (Wang et al., 2009) by turning off the entire SO together, instead of only the output stage, with its common mode feedback (CMFB) circuit, the power consumption of the SO can be reduced about 50%.

2.3.2 Op-amp less

The traditional way of designing analogue circuits relies on high gain op-amps in negative feedback loops. As it was stated before, the op-amp power consumption directly impacts in the overall system. Recently, there is the trend of replacing the op-amps by more power efficient blocks such as comparators, inverters or simple structures based on local feedback. In this section, some of these approaches are described to illustrate this trend.

CBSC (Comparator Based Switched Capacitors) and zero-crossing detector based circuits

The CBSC technique was firstly proposed in (Fiorenza et al., 2006) and is applicable to any traditional op-amp based SC circuit. This technique consists in replacing the op-amp by a comparator and one or more switched current sources. As the author explains, the power reduction relies in the fact that a CBSC circuit senses the virtual ground while in traditional op-amp based SC circuit the virtual ground is forced which is less energy efficient.

Several ADC prototypes have demonstrated the practical application of CBSS and its potential high energy efficiency. In (Shin et al. 2008), a 10 bits pipelined ADC based in zero-crossing detector fabricated using 65nm CMOS technology is reported.

Another pipelined zero-crossing detector based is presented in (Brooks & Lee, 2009). It achieves 12 bits of ENOB sampling at 50MS/s with high power efficiency indicated by a FOM of 88fJ/step.

Inverter based $\Delta\Sigma$ modulators

This technique is another approach in which the op-amp is replaced by a simple inverter, which can be considered as a very simplified amplifier architecture. In the past, inverters had been applied to SC circuits as low-performance amplifiers for micropower consumption (Hosticka, 1979). In spite of the limited performance of inverters compared with op-amps, inverters attract attention again to be used in deep submicron technologies. This is because of their ability to operate with very low supply voltages. Recent works have demonstrated that inverter-based design techniques can be applicable to high-performance SC circuits in aggressively scaled CMOS technologies.

For example, (van Veldhoven et al., 2008) present a hybrid $\Sigma\Delta$ modulator fabricated in 65nm CMOS technology. It uses a highly digitized architecture with a five bits quantizer and a digital filter in order to reduce the complexity of the feedback DAC. A first order analogue loop filter (implemented using inverters) reduces the analogue parts to the minimum, so the area and power consumption are drastically reduced.

In (Chae & Han, 2009) the inverter behaviour used as an extremely simple amplifier is explained in detail. Three discrete time (DT) $\Delta\Sigma$ modulators of second and third order completely implemented by means of inverters are presented in this work. All of them achieve high dynamic range under low voltage supply conditions with a power consumption that places the best of them in the state-of-the-art nowadays.

Simple analogue cells based in local feedback

Simple local feedback can lead to substantial enhancement of the performance with low cost in terms of noise, area and power consumption as it is usually implemented by a simple structure.

One good example is the structure called the Flipped Voltage Follower (FVF), a popular building block that relies on the local feedback idea. It was proposed in (Carvajal et al., 2005) to improve the performance of the classical voltage follower by means of local feedback.

A very commonly implemented basic cell in analogue microelectronics is the voltage follower (Fig. 1a). However, the gate-to-source voltage (v_{GS}) of the transistor acting as the follower (M1) depends on the output current, which leads to a high distortion for large output current variations. Some solutions have been proposed to address this problem (Sánchez-Sinencio & Silva-Martínez, 2000), (Barthélemy & Kussener, 2001), (Carvajal et al., 2005). The FVF is the basic cell made up by transistors M_1 and M_2 and the current source I_B shown in Fig. 1b. The local feedback implemented by transistor M_2 keeps constant the current through transistor M_1; this decreases the output impedance increasing the linearity of the current copy and in spite of output current variations.

A modified version of the FVF was proposed in (Luján et al., 2011) showing a better performance for large excursions of the input signal up to 10MHz and allowing a reduction in the quiescent power consumption of about 15 times when comparing with the classical solution, for the same linearity performances.

The idea of using local feedback to maintain the linearity requirements, while the power consumption is decreased, can be extended to more complex systems such as ADCs. One example of this is the CT $\Sigma\Delta$ modulator described in the section 3.2 of this chapter. A low power extremely low area CT $\Sigma\Delta$ modulator implementation based on the FVF is explained.

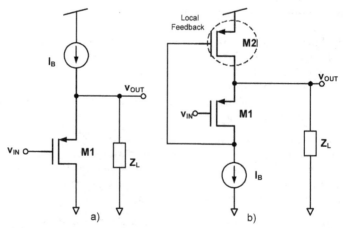

Fig. 1. Voltage followers: a) classical solution and b) FVF.

Other op-amp-less approaches

Another example of a simplified op-amp-less architecture is the ADC array (Draxelmayr, 2004). Using parallelism to exploit the power efficiency of simple structures, a 6-bit ADC working at 600 MS/s based on eight SAR ADCs using a charge redistribution architecture is proposed. A power consumption of only 10 mW is obtained with very simple analogue circuitry (capacitors, switches and a comparator are sufficient) and no need for "precision" analogue blocks, like high gain op-amps.

In (Van der Plas, 2006) a 4-bit flash scheme with a comparator based simplified structure is proposed to design a high speed low-power ADC. Its structure is reduced to save power by removing all the non essential blocks: Track &Hold, preamplifiers, reference ladder and bubble error correction. A comparator circuit combining sampling, amplification and reference level generation is used to implement the ADC obtaining a power consumption of only 2.5 mW.

2.4 Efficient use of biasing

Charge transfer in class-A op-amp circuitry is inherently inefficient; the amplifier is biased with a constant current, while delivering on average only a small fraction of this current to the load. In this section, a more efficient use of biasing is discussed and various approaches adopted to solve this problem are commented.

2.4.1 Dynamic and adaptive biasing

In the last decades, several approaches have been proposed to optimize the efficient use of biasing towards the challenge of minimizing the power consumption-performance ratio. Most of them can be classified according to the concepts of dynamic and adaptive biasing. The term *dynamic biasing* was first coined in (Copeland & Rabaey, 1979), where a method to reduce the power consumption by taking advantage of having several clock phases in a SC integrator was proposed. This method is valid for all those circuits where there is a capacitive feedback between the output and a virtual ground.

Since then, the concept of dynamic biasing has been extended, in general, to those approaches in which a block or part of it is connected or disconnected according to the received input power. An example of this technique is proposed in (Ozun et al., 2006) where a parallel combination of transconductors is used, increasing the power consumption only if very low noise is required.

At the same time, the term of *adaptive biasing* (Degrauwe et al., 1981) has also become popular. It is usually referred to a continuous time change in the biasing according to the input. One of the most important adaptive biasing techniques is the class AB operation. In this technique, the slew rate limitation is tackled by boosting automatically dynamic tail currents for large inputs, keeping a well-controlled low quiescent current (Degrauwe et al., 1981) , (Callewaert & Sansen, 1990), (Castello & Gray, 1985), (Tan & Chen, 2007), (Klinke et al., 1989), (Harjani et al., 1999).

Several schemes can be found in the literature for class AB operation amplifiers. Most of them require of additional circuitry, which increases both power consumption and active area. Often they also imply additional parasitic capacitances to the internal nodes

(Degrauwe et al., 1981), degrading the small signal performance of the circuit which is already poor due to the low quiescent current. In some cases, the stability issues get worse due to the use of positive feedback or structures that are sensitive to variations in process and environmental parameters (Callewaert & Sansen, 1990), (Klinke et al., 1989). Although other contributions consider negative feedback (Harjani et al., 1999), the required additional amplifiers to implement the feedback loops lead to complex designs. Another weakness of the tail current boosting topologies is that usually are not suitable for low voltage applications as in (Castello & Gray, 1985) due to the stacking of gate to source voltages.

Recently, some topologies based in the FVF (López-Martín et al., 2009) or using "Quasi" Floating Gate (QFG) techniques have been proposed (Ramírez-Angulo et al., 2006), while the first one offers simplicity of design and suitability for low-voltage operation simultaneously to high efficiency; the second one also minimizes the additional circuitry required just substituting a normal MOS transistor by a QFG MOS.

Class AB operation can be applied to the input, to the output or both. This last option is known as superclass AB operation (López-Martín et al., 2005). The concept of class AB operation is so spread that today we can talk, for instance, about Class AB DACs (Seo et al., 2009), Sample & Holds (Sawigun & Serdjin, 2011) and multipliers (Sawigun & Serdijn, 2009) among others.

2.4.2 Assisted op-amp and helper techniques

Instead of removing op-amps, as it has been explained in section 2.3.2, a less aggressive technique consists in keeping the op-amp but adding helper circuits that increase the energy efficiency by relaxing the requirements for the op-amp gain or bandwidth.

For instance, in (Musah et al. 2007) the concept of correlated level shifting (CLS) is introduced. Correlated double sampling (CDS) technique can be used to reduce the error caused by finite open-loop gain, but it limits the maximum speed and its performance is poor near the rails. This makes it unsuitable for low voltage conditions, since the voltage swing is reduced too much. CLS is a SC technique similar to CDS, which also decreases the errors due to finite open-loop gain and allows rail-to-rail operation increasing the "distortion-free" swing. A third clock phase is needed but the settling time is about the same, so it does not have impact on the circuit speed. Open-loop gain requirements can be relaxed for a given resolution, leading to power consumption saving.

Another approach of op-amp helper is the assisted op-amp technique proposed in (Pavan et al. 2010). It is well known that the op-amp in the first integrator of high resolution single-bit CT $\Sigma\Delta$ modulators has stringent slew rate requirements, increasing power dissipation. In CT single bit $\Sigma\Delta$ modulators the feedback DAC injects a very high frequency current signal at the virtual ground node of the op-amp which the first integrator is implemented with. If the op-amp is not fast enough, this high frequency signal produces strong variations at the virtual ground node which result in distortion. The conventional way of addressing this issue is to bias the op-amps with large currents, so that the bandwidth and slew rate of the op-amp are enhanced. This work introduces the "assisted op-amp" integrator, which offers a way of relaxing the speed specifications of the op-amp in the first integrator, achieving low distortion operation with low power consumption.

3. Applications examples

In this section, two examples of design which make use of some of the previous power reduction techniques are presented. Firstly, the design of an active-RC channel filter for ULPBT applications is explained. It achieves micro-power consumption by using an efficient class-AB op-amp biased in the weak inversion region. Then, the design of an efficient op-amp less implementation for CT $\Sigma\Delta$ modulators is described. In the proposed implementation, the op-amp is replaced by the compact local feedback structure explained in section 2.3.2.

3.1 Micropower active-RC channel filter for a Zero-IF Ultra Low Power Bluetooth receiver

In the case of the low-power RC filter and in order to reduce the power consumption, an adaptive biasing technique has been used. Specifically, a new topology of class-AB op-amp has been used so that the current consumption is adapted to the output requirements. The designed filter will be used in the ULPBT receiver based on a Zero-IF architecture like the one shown in Fig. 2. The main challenge of this design is the implementation of an efficient low-pass channel filter meeting the stringent demands of the receiver.

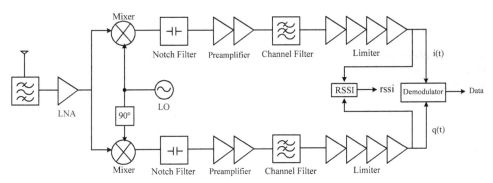

Fig. 2. Zero-IF receiver architecture for Ultra Low Power Bluetooth Standard.

An active RC topology has been chosen to implement the filter. Sallen-Key (SK) and multifeedback (MFB) topologies are usually employed in this kind of filters. Both architectures are attractive for low power design, since they comprise an active element per biquad performing at the same time low noise and high linearity. The main drawback of active RC filters for low power design is the high op-amp bandwidth required. The power consumption is optimized by using class-AB two-stage op-amp with enhanced gain and rail-to-rail output swing.

Based on the overall receiver planning, the low pass filter should provide a gain of 10 dB with a cut-off frequency of 1 MHz and a noise figure of less than 50 dB. According to the required stop-band attenuation of 45 dB at 3 MHz, a fourth-order Butterworth filter meets the requirements.

The topology of the active RC filter is shown in Fig. 3. It has been implemented by two biquadratic sections in cascade. Several combinations of second-order sections connected in cascade have been studied to fulfil the requirements for noise and op-amp bandwidth.

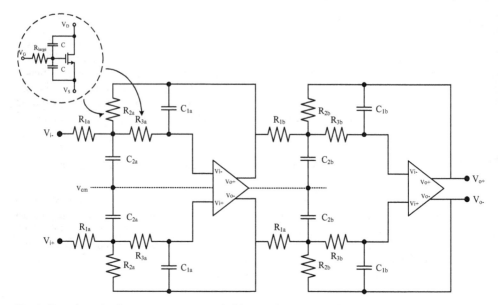

Fig. 3. Fourth-order low pass Butterworth filter with MFB topology.

The low voltage environment of this work (1.2 V power supply) leads to an amplifier topology that should provide rail-to-rail output swing. This fact precludes the use of cascode transistors to increase the voltage gain. In this context, two-stage op-amps are the natural choice, since they have rail-to-rail output swing and can drive both resistive and capacitive loads. In active RC topologies, the high op-amp bandwidth required (the op-amp unity-gain bandwidth has to be much larger than the filter pole) leads easily to high power consumption.

The fully balanced two-stage amplifier is shown in Fig. 4. This topology can provide rail-to-rail operation with better power efficiency than a Miller amplifier since the conventional two-stage amplifier needs a compensation capacitor to ensure the stability, and additional current to drive this capacitance. The main drawback is the low voltage gain. The operational amplifier often consumes large power to obtain a high gain. However, in this case, the gain is increased by placing two current sources M_{4a} and M_{4b} in parallel with the diode-connected transistors. In this design, the current of transistors M_{4a} and M_{4b} has been set at $k(I_{bias}/2)$ where the k factor is 0.8, boosting the gain $1/(1 - k)$ times (Steyaert et al., 1991; Yao et al., 2004).

For minimum power consumption and large current drive capability, one of the techniques explained in this chapter, the class-AB operation is used. Class AB output stages generate output currents larger than the output stage quiescent current. The class-AB performance of the output stage is achieved, without additional current, including a large resistive element implemented using a minimum size diode connected PMOS transistor M_{Rlarge} and a small capacitor C_{bat} (Ramírez-Angulo et al., 2006). The value of C_{bat} can be small, as transistor M_{Rlarge} is intended to operate as a very large resistive element. Under quiescent conditions and given that no DC current flows through M_{Rlarge} the voltage at the gate of M_{6b} is the same as at the gate of M_{bias} so that the quiescent current in M_{bias} and M_{6b} has the same value I_{bias}. During dynamic operation, when the output of the op-amp is slewing, the voltage at node X

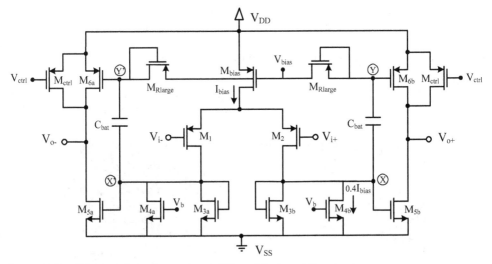

Fig. 4. Fully differential single-stage amplifier with class-AB output.

is subject to a large change. Given that capacitor C_{bat} cannot charge or discharge rapidly through M_{Rlarge}, it acts as a floating battery and transfers the voltage variations at node X to node Y. This provides class AB (push–pull) operation to the output stage. No additional circuitry to control the desired value of the quiescent output current is necessary due to the large resistor.

A conventional CMFB circuit is incorporated to control the output voltage. The output stage has low supply requirements since it can operate with a voltage close to the threshold voltage of a transistor: $V_{DD}^{min} = V_{GS,5b} + V_{SDsat,2} + V_{SDsat,bias}$.

The biasing current of the op-amp is 20 μA. The current through transistors M_4 is adjusted at $0.4I_{bias}$ and M_5 size is ten times larger than M_3 size. The CMFB consumes 20 μA. Thus the total supply current is 80 μA.

Due to process variations, integrated components can differ significantly from their nominal values. In order to compensate for these variations, RC-opamp filters must be tuneable. A switched array of passive resistors and/or capacitors and MOSFET-C technique are usually employed. The latter is the simplest way and features continuous programmability. Passive resistors are replaced by MOSFET operated in triode region and the gate voltage is tuned to make the filter parameters programmable.

In this work, the device coined as "quasi" floating gate MOS (Ramírez-Angulo et al., 2003) is used to replace the passive resistors. A QFG MOS transistor consists of a MOS transistor with capacitive gate voltage averaging biased using a large resistive element R_{large} (Ramírez-Angulo et al., 2004), as shown in Fig. 3. for resistances R_{2a} and R_{3a}. The large resistance R_{large} for QFG MOS resistors has been implemented using MOS transistors operating in subthreshold region (Bikumandla et al., 2004), since the resistance of a transistor operating in this region is very large (tens of GΩ). Transistors operate in subthreshold region with a bias current I_{subth} of 10 nA. This method to implement programmable linear resistors improves the linearity at the cost of increasing the area, mainly due to the use of two capacitors (C in Fig. 3). In order to save area, resistors R_1 are implemented by polysilicon ensuring a linear V–I conversion. Resistors R_2 and R_3 will be tuned to control the main parameters of the filter: gain, quality factor and cut-off frequency.

The proposed fourth-order Butterworth filter has been fabricated in a 0.18 μm CMOS technology. Figure 5 shows the chip microphotograph. The active area of the chip is 0.45 mm x 0.27 mm = 0.12 mm² and it is dominated by the capacitors. The filter operates with a single 1.2 V supply voltage.

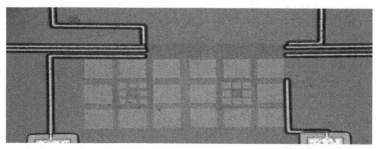

Fig. 5. Filter microphotograph.

Figure 6a illustrates the measured frequency tuning around the nominal frequency of 1 MHz. The cut-off frequency can be tuned from 800 kHz to 1.3 MHz. The measured two-tone intermodulation distortion for the filter is shown in Fig .6b. In this measurement, the cut-off frequency of the filter was set to the nominal value of 1 MHz. The frequencies of the input tones are at 500 and 600 kHz and the third intermodulation (IM3) products are at 400 and 700 kHz. Note that the IM3 of the filter is -46.8 dB, the noise figure is 46 dB and the input noise 85 nV/√Hz, which is approximately 85 μV in the 3 dB passband. Low noise behaviour is achieved in a low power environment mainly due to the use of only two amplifiers.

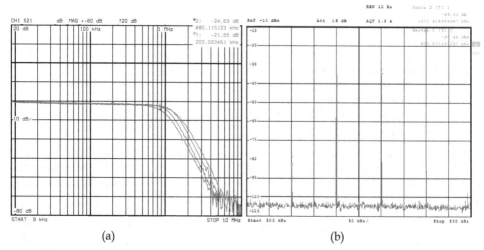

(a)   (b)

Fig. 6. (a) Measured filter frequency response (b) Measured IM3 for the proposed filter.

A summary of the experimental results is given in Table 1.

Supply Voltage	1.2 V
Technology	0.18 μm CMOS
Silicon Area	0.12 mm^2
Transfer Function	Fourth-order Butterworth
Cut-off Frequency	1 MHz
Frequency tuning range	800 KHz - 1.3 MHz
DC Gain	10 dB
IIP3	16 dBm
Input-referred noise	85 μV
Static Power Consumption	290 μW

Table 1. Summary of experimental results.

3.2 Compact op-amp less CT ΣΔ modulator implementation for passive RFID applications

Combining sensors with passive RFID tags opens the way for new applications such as automotive and healthcare. As the passive RFID sensor nodes are intended to be powered by energy scavenging, ultra-low power consumption and robustness against process variations and changes in the supply voltage are essential requirements. In addition, low area occupancy is crucial in order to decrease the fabrication costs.

Low-bandwidth, moderate-resolution ADCs consuming a few microwatts are key elements for the sensor interface. Successive approximation register (SAR) converters are the typical choice for moderate-resolution low-frequency applications with ultra-low power requirements such as passive RFID. This type of converter achieves moderate resolution with very low power consumption and sets the state-of-the art in terms of energy efficiency. However, they consume large active area as the required DAC is normally implemented by a capacitor network. In this work the CT ΣΔ modulator architecture is proposed as an alternative to SAR architecture when the application also requires from very low area occupancy. CT ΣΔ modulators have become very popular over the last years, especially for lower power applications.

Traditionally, the loop filter is implemented either using an active-RC integrator or a gm-C approach. As it has been explained in the section 2 of this chapter, recent trends in low-power ADC design replace the internal op-amps (which usually are the most power consuming building blocks) with simple analogue circuitry. Following this trend, in this work a novel CT ΣΔ modulator implementation based on a local feedback is presented. The feedback provides a virtual ground node for reference subtraction without the need of op-amps or Operational Transconductance Amplifiers (OTAs). A first-order ΣΔ modulator prototype with low complexity at system level and minimum area occupancy has been designed in order to validate the idea.

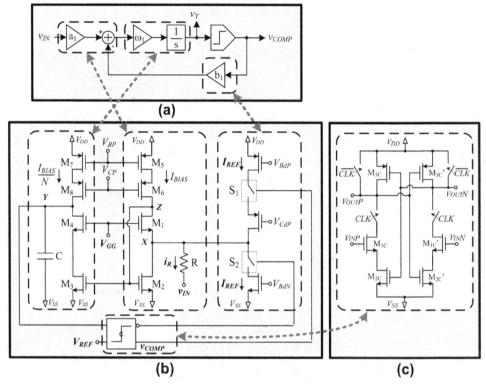

Fig. 7. First-order CT single-bit $\Sigma\Delta$ modulator. (a) Block diagram, (b) Proposed implementation, (c) Comparator schematic.

In Fig .7a the block diagram of a typical first-order CT single-bit $\Sigma\Delta$ modulator is shown. The modulator is made up of a comparator and a CT loop filter, which performs the subtraction and integration, as expressed in equation (1).

$$v_Y(s) = \omega_1 \frac{a_1 v_{IN}(s) - b_1 v_{COMP}(s)}{s} \tag{2}$$

The compact implementation shown in Fig 7.b is proposed, where the input stage, the integrator stage and the feedback DAC have been highlighted.

The input voltage, v_{IN} is converted into a current i_R by means of resistor R which connects the input signal to node X. Thanks to the feedback loop built up with transistors $M1$ and $M2$ and current source I_{BIAS}, the equivalent resistance at node X is extremely low.

In order to close the $\Sigma\Delta$ feedback loop the comparator controls two switches, S_1 and S_2, so that a reference current I_{REF} is injected or subtracted at node X depending on the comparator output. Therefore, the subtraction between the input signal and the comparator output is performed at node X in current mode. Note that both functions, the input voltage-to-current conversion and the feedback signal subtraction, are carried out by one resistor, two transistors and a current source. Then, the resulting current is copied and integrated in a capacitor.

By a proper selection of V_{GG}, so that the quiescent value of the input voltage ($V_{IN}{}^Q$) is equal to the bias voltage of node X ($V_X{}^Q$), the drain current of transistor M2 is given by:

$$i_{D,M2} = I_{BIAS} + \frac{v_{in} + V_{IN}^Q - V_X^Q}{R} \pm I_{REF} = I_{BIAS} + \frac{v_{IN}}{R} \pm I_{REF} \qquad (3)$$

As the input voltage is converted to current by a linear resistor, having a very low impedance at node X is crucial to achieve a good linearity at the input stage. This requirement is achieved thanks to the local feedback that keeps constant the current through transistor M1 in spite of output current variations at node X. Neglecting the body effect, the input impedance at node X is given by (Carvajal et al., 2005)

$$r_X = \frac{r_{o2}}{1 + g_{m1}r_{o2} + g_{m1}g_{m2}r_{o1}r_{o2}} \approx \frac{1}{g_{m1}g_{m2}r_{o1}}$$

which, for typical parameter values in the selected technology, is low enough to guarantee the linearity requirements for this application.

The current at the drain of M2, $i_{D,M2}$, is copied to node Y by the current mirror implemented with transistors M3 and M4, where the current I_{BIAS} is removed. The resulting current is injected into capacitor C where the integration is carried out. Finally, the voltage at node Y is given by (in the s-Domain):

$$v_Y(s) = \frac{v_{IN}(s)}{RCs} \mp \frac{I_{REF}}{Cs} \qquad (4)$$

Expressions (2) and (4) are equivalent if $a_1\omega_1=1/RC$ and $b_1\omega_1 V_{COMP}=I_{REF}/C$. Note that no additional circuitry is required to bias the node Y. To reduce power consumption, the current through M3 (and M7) can be downscaled by modifying the gain of the current mirror. In our implementation a ratio of N=3 was chosen.

To save power, the dynamic latch-type comparator show in Fig .7c has been selected to close the modulator loop. Two switches open the latch branches during the reset phase so that the quiescent current consumption is zero.

To verify the proper operation of the proposed implementation, a first-order CT $\Sigma\Delta$ modulator prototype has been fabricated. The modulator digitalizes the signal coming from a MEMS accelerometer, which is a single-ended structure presently available in a 0.35μm CMOS technology. The ADC will be integrated in the same die with the MEMS accelerometer so it was designed in the same technology and with a single-ended input. The whole system is intended to be powered by an UHF RFID front-end which provides a 3V nominal supply voltage typical for the selected technology (Vaz et al., 2010). Fig. 8a shows a microphotograph of the fabricated prototype. The total area consumption (without pads) is only 110μm x 125μm for the whole proposed circuit which makes it, to the author's knowledge, the smallest $\Sigma\Delta$ modulator published for this range of specifications.

The measured output spectrum for a 7.85kHz sinusoidal input signal is shown in Fig. 8b. A peak SNDR (Signal-to-Noise plus Distortion Ratio) of 49dB has been obtained for a -5dBFS input signal. Fig .8c shows the measured SNR/SNDR versus input signal amplitude. It can be seen that the prototype achieves 56dB of Dynamic Range (DR), which means about 9 bits of ENOB over a 25kHz signal bandwidth. Experimental results are summarized in Table 2.

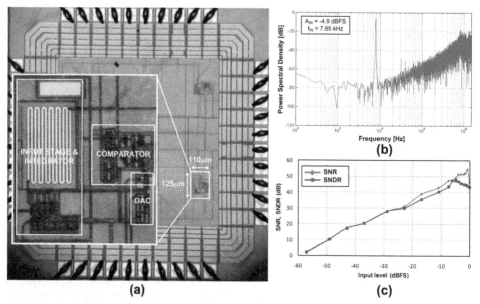

Fig. 8. (a) Circuit microphotograph, (b) Measured output spectrum, (c) SNR/SNDR versus input signal amplitude. Input signal frequency = 7.85 kHz. V_{DD} = 3V.

The designed modulator has also shown to be very robust against supply voltage and bias current variations. The DR remains over 52dB for a supply voltage variation in the range 2.25 to 5 volts even for a 50% decrease of nominal bias current.

The FOM defined by (5) has been used to have an estimation of the energy efficiency achieved by the proposed $\Sigma\Delta$ modulator implementation. The minimum power consumption

Sampling frequency (MHz)	3.2
Signal Bandwidth (kHz)	25
Oversampling ratio	64
Peak SNR (dB)	54.5 (@7.85kHz)
Peak SNDR (dB)	49 (@7.85kHz)
Dynamic range (dB)	56.2
ENOB (bit)	9.04
Input range (mVpp)	700
Power consumption (µW)	4.35 (@Vdd=2.25V)
Power supply (V)	3
PSRR (dB)	32
Vdd for ENOB > 7bits (V)	2.25 to 5
Active area (mm²)	0.01375
Technology	AMS 0.35µm CMOS

Table 2. Summary of measured modulator performances.

(4.35μW) was measured for a 2.25V supply voltage, leading to a FOM of 0.267 pJ/step. This value places this work close to the most power efficient CT ΣΔ modulators recently published, despite that it has been implemented in a reasonable old technology.

$$FOM = \frac{P}{2^{ENOB} \cdot 2BW} \tag{5}$$

Fig. 9a gives a graphical representation of the state-of-the-art of power efficient ADCs in the same range of bandwidth. The measured performance of the proposed implementation is competitive in terms of energy efficiency compared with the state-of-the-art. The SAR converter (Harpe et al., 2010) sets the state-of-the-art and only a few ΣΔ modulators perform better than the proposed in this work.

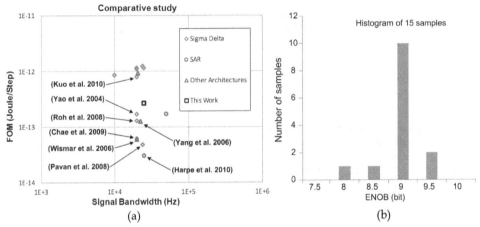

(a)   (b)

Fig. 9. (a) State of the art of ADCs regarding the selected FOM. (b) ENOB deviation for 15 measured samples (second version of the converter, V_{DD} = 3V, input signal frequency = 7.85 kHz.

Fig. 9b shows a histogram of the ENOB deviation for 15 samples fabricated. Every sample worked properly with an ENOB variation lower than than ±0.5 bits, which is an indication of the robustness of the proposed modulator implementation against the process variation.

A compact implementation for CT ΣΔ modulators based on a local feedback has been presented. In order to validate the idea, a first order CT ΣΔ modulator for a self powered sensor interface (9-bits of resolution and 25-kHz of signal bandwidth) has been designed in a 0.35μm CMOS technology. Experimental results confirm the idea and show that the proposed implementation leads to an extremely low area and highly power efficient ΣΔ modulator. The measured prototype has also shown to be very robust against process, supply voltage and bias current variations.

4. Conclusions

In this chapter, the need of minimizing power consumption in electronic devices has been pointed out. For this reason, a review of the most common techniques used by IC designers with this purpose has been done. These techniques have been classified in four categories: biasing point optimization, digitally assisted techniques, analogue circuitry simplification and efficient use of biasing. In order to illustrate the large number of techniques that these categories involve, several references have been proposed through the chapter. Furthermore, two approaches based on the use of some of the reported techniques have been described. The first one proposes a micropower active-RC channel filter for an Ultra Low Power Bluetooth Receiver based on a zero-IF architecture. It uses a new topology of class-AB op-amp so that the current consumption is adapted to the output requirements. The second design proposes a compact op-amp less CT ΣΔ modulator for passive RFID applications. In order to reduce the power consumption, a local feedback technique is used.

5. Acknowledgment

This work was supported in part by the Spanish Ministry of Science and Technology and in part by the Andalusian Regional Government under Projects TEC2010-21563-C02-02 and TIC-6323-2011, respectively.

6. References

Allen, P. E. & Holberg, D. R. (2002). *CMOS Analog Circuit Design* (2), Oxford Univ. Press, ISBN: 0195116445, New York.

Barthélemy, H. & Kussener, E., (2001), High speed voltage follower for standard BICMOS technology, *IEEE Transactions on Circuits and Systems II: Analog and Digital Signal Processing*. Vol. 48, No.7, (July 2001), pp. (727-732). ISSN 1057-7130.

Belleville, M. ; Fanet, H.; Fiorini, P.; Nicole, P.; Pelgrom, M.J.M.; Piguet, C.; Hahn, R.; VanHoof, C.; Vullers, R.; Tartagni, M. & Cantatore, E. (2010). Energy autonomous sensor systems: Towards a ubiquitous sensor technology. *Elsevier Microelectronics Journal*. Vol., No. 41, (March 2010), pp.(740-745).

Bikumandla, M.; Ramírez-Angulo, J.; Urquidi, C. A.; González-Carvajal, R. & López-Martín, A. J. (2004). Biasing CMOS amplifiers using MOS transistors in subthreshold region, *IEICE Electronics Express*, Vol. 1, No. 12, (September 2004), pp. (339–345).

Binkley, D. M.; Hopper, C. E.; Tucker, S. D.; Moss, B. C.; Rochelle, J. M. & Foty, D. P (2003). A CAD methodology for optimizing transistor current and sizing in analog CMOS design. *IEEE Transactions on Computer-Aided Design of Integrated Circuits and Systems*, Vol. 22, No. 2, (February 2003), pp. (225–237).

Borkar, S. (1999). Design challenges of technology scaling. *IEEE Micro*, Vol.19, No.4, Jul-Aug 1999, pp. (23-29).

Brooks, L. and Hae-Seung Lee; (2009). *A 12b 50MS/s fully differential zero-crossing-based ADC without CMFB*, IEEE International Solid-State Circuits Conference - Digest of Technical Papers, ISSCC 2009, (8-12 Feb. 2009), pp.(166 - 167).

Callewaert, L.G.A. & Sansen, W.M.C (1990). Class AB CMOS amplifiers with high efficiency, *IEEE Journal of Solid-State Circuits*. Vol. 25, No.3, (June 1990), pp. (684-691). ISSN 0018-9200.

Cao, Z.; Yan, S. & Li, Y. A 32 mW 1.25 GS/s 6b 2b/Step SAR ADC in 0.13 μm CMOS. IEEE Journal of Solid State Circuits, vol. 44, nª 3, March 2009, pp. (862-873).

Carvajal, R. G.; Ramírez-Angulo, A. J.; Torralba, A.; Gómez Galán, J. A.; Carlosena, A & Muñoz-Chavero, F. (2005), The Flipped Voltage Follower: A useful cell for low-power low-voltage design, *IEEE Transactions on Circuits and Systems I: Regular Papers.* Vol. 52, No.7, (July 2005), pp.(1276-1291), ISSN 1549-8328.

Casson, A.J. and Rodriguez-Villegas, E. *A 60 pW gm-C Continuous Wavelet Transform Circuit for Portable EEG Systems.* IEEE Journal of Solid-State Circuits, Vol.46, No.6, (June 2011), pp.(1406-1415).

Castello, R. & Gray, P.R. (1985). A high-performance micropower switched-capacitor filter, *IEEE Journal of Solid-State Circuits.* Vol.20, No.6, (December 1985), pp. (1122- 1132). ISSN 0018-9200.

Chae, Y. and Han. G (2009). *Low Voltage, Low Power, Inverter-Based Switched-Capacitor Delta-Sigma Modulator.* IEEE J. Solid-State Circuits, Vo. 44 , No. 2, (Jan. 2009), pp. (458 - 472).

Chanapromma, C.; Silapan, P.; Duangmalai, D. & Siripruchyanun, M. (2010). An Ultra Low-Power Fully Differential Operational Transconductance Amplifier (FD-OTA) operating in Weak-Inversion Region and Its Applications, *Proceedings of the 1st International Conference on Technical Education, ICTE2009,* (January 2010), pp. (176-179).

Colodro, P. ; Torralba, A. & Laguna, M. Continuous-Time Sigma–Delta Modulator With an Embedded Pulsewidth Modulation. *IEEE Trans. on Circuits and Systems-I,* vol. 55, Issue 3, March 2008, pp. (775-785).

Comer, D. J. & Comer, D. T (2004). Using the weak inversion region to optimize input stage design of op amps. *IEEE Transactions on Circuits and Systems II,* Vol. 51, No. 1, (January 2004), pp. (8–14).

Comer, D. J. & Comer, D. T (2004). Operation of analog MOS circuits in the weak or moderate inversion region. *IEEE Transactions on Education,* Vol. 47, No. 4, (November 2004), pp. (430–435).

Copeland, M. A. & Rabaey, J.M., E. (1979). Dynamic amplifier for m.o.s. technology. *Electronic Letters.* Vol. 15, No. 10, (May 2010), pp. (301-302). ISSN 0013-5194.

Corbishley, P. & Rodríguez-Villegas, E. (2007). A Nanopower Bandpass Filter for Detection of an Acoustic Signal in a Wearable Breathing Detector, *IEEE Transactions On Biomedical Circuits and Systems,* Vol. 1, No. 3, (September 2007), pp. (163-171).

Degrauwe, M.; Rijmenants, J.; Vittoz, E. & De Man, H. (1981). CMOS Adaptive Biasing Amplifier. *Proceedings of the European Solid State Circuits Conference, ESSCIRC 1981,* ISBN: 3800712385, Freiburg, September 1981.

Draxelmayr, D. A 6b 600MHz 10mW ADC Array in Digital 90nm CMOS. Digest of Technical Papers of IEEE International Solid-State Circuits Conference 2004, February 2004.

Enz, C. C.; Krummenacher, F. & Vittoz, E. A (1995). An analytical MOS transistor model valid in all regions of operation and dedicated to low voltage and low-current applications, *Analog Integr. Circuits Signal Process. J.,* Vol. 8, (July 1995), pp. (83–114).

Farshidi, E. & Alaei-sheini, N. (2009). A Micropower Current-Mode Sigma-Delta Modulator for Biomedical Applications, *IEEE Signal Processing and Communications Applications Conference, SIU 2009,* (2009), pp. (856-859).

Fiorenza, J. K.; Sepke, T.; Holloway, P.; Sodini, C. G. and Lee, H.-S. (2006). *Comparator-based switched-capacitor circuits for scaled CMOS technologies,* IEEE J. Solid-State Circuits, Vol. 41, (Dec. 2006), pp. (2658–2668).

Flynn, M. P. ; Donovan, C. & Satler, L. Digital calibration incorporating redundancy of Flash ADCs. *IEEE Transactions on Circuits and Systems II,* vol. 50, n° 5, May 2003, pp. (205-213).

Gray, P. R.; Hurst, P. J.; Lewis, S. H. & Meyer, R. G. (2001). *Analysis and Design of Analog Integrated Circuits.* Wiley, ISBN: 0471321680, New York.

Harjani, R.; Heineke, R. & Feng W. (1999). An integrated low-voltage class AB CMOS OTA, *IEEE Journal of Solid-State Circuits*. Vol.34, No.2, (February 1999), pp.(134-142). ISSN 0018-9200.

Harpe, P.; Cui Zhou; Xiaoyan Wang; Dolmans, G and de Groot, H. (2010). *A 30fJ/conversion-step 8b 0-to-10MS/s asynchronous SAR ADC in 90nm CMOS*, ISSCC Dig. Tech. Papers, (7-11 Feb. 2010), pp. (388-389).

Hashemi, S. & Shoaei, O.; A 0.9-V 10-bit 100-MSample/s pipelined ADC using switched-RC and opamp sharing techniques. *50th Midwest Symposium on Circuits and Systems 2007*, Aug. 2007.

Hosticka, B. J. (1979). *Dynamic CMOS amplifiers*, IEEE J. Solid-State Circuits, Vol. 14, (Dec. 1979) , pp. (1111–1114).

Jimenez-Irastorza, A.; Sevillano, J.F.; Berenguer, R. and Rebollo, I. (2011). *Recursive Successive Approximation Time-to-Digital Converter for low-power RFID tag sensors*, XXVI Conference on Design of Circuits and Integrated Systems (DCIS), (November 2011).

Kijima, M.; Ito, K.; Kamei, K. & Tsukamoto, S. A 6b 3GS/s Flash ADC with Background Calibration. *Proceedings of IEEE 2009 Custom Intergrated Circuits Conference*, San Jose, CA, September 2009.

Kim, H.-C.; Jeong, D.-K. & Kim, W. A partially switched-opamp technique for high-speed low-power pipelined analog-to-digital converters. *IEEE Transactions on Circuits and Systems I: Regular Papers*, vol.53, no.4, April 2006, pp. (795- 801).

Klinke, R.; Hosticka, B.J. & Pfleiderer, H. (1989). A very-high-slew-rate CMOS operational amplifier, *IEEE Journal of Solid-State Circuits*. Vol.24, No.3, (June 1989), pp. (744-746). ISSN 0018-9200.

Kuo, C.-H. & Liu, S.-H. A 1-V 10.7-MHz Fourth-Order Bandpass $\Sigma\Delta$ Modulators Using Two Switched Opamps. *IEEE Journal of Solid-State Circuits*, vol. 39, n^a 11, November 2004, pp. (2041-2045).

Kuo, C-H.; Shi, D-Y. & Chang K-S. (2010). A Low-Voltage Fourth-Order Cascade Delta-Sigma Modulator in 0.18-μm CMOS. *IEEE Transactions on Circuits and Systems I: Regular Papers*, Vol. 57, No. 9, (Sept. 2010), pp.(2450-2461).

López-Martín, A.J.; Baswa, S.; Ramirez-Angulo, J & Carvajal, R.G. (2005). Low-Voltage Super class AB CMOS OTA cells with very high slew rate and power efficiency, *IEEE Journal of Solid-State Circuits*. Vol.40, No.5, (May 2005), pp. (1068- 1077). ISSN 0018-9200.

López-Martín, A.J.; Ramirez-Angulo, J.; Carvajal, R.G. & Acosta, L. (2009). Power-efficient class AB CMOS buffer, *Electronics Letters*. Vol.45, No.2, (January 2009), pp. (89-90). ISSN 0013-5194.

Luján, C.I.; Torralba, A.; Carvajal, R.G.; Ramírez-Angulo, J. (2011), Highly linear voltage follower based on local feedback and cascode transistor with dynamic biasing, *Electronics Letters*, Vol.47, No.4, (February 2011) pp.244-246. ISSN 0013-5194.

Markovic, D.; Wang, C. C.; Alarcon, L. P.; Tsung-Te, Liu & Rabaey, J. M (2010). Ultralow-Power Design in Near-Threshold Region. *Proceedings of the IEEE*, Vol. 98, No. 2, (February 2010), pp. (237-252).

Murmann, B. (2008). A/D Converter Trends: Power Dissipation, Scaling and Digitally Assisted Architectures. *Proceedings of IEEE Custom Integrated Circuits Conference, 2008, CICC 2008*. ISBN 978-1-4244-2018-6, San Jose, CA, November 2008.

Musah, T.; Gregoire, B.R.; Naviasky, E. and Moon, U.-K. (2007). Parallel correlated double sampling technique for pipelined analogue-to-digital converters, *Electronics Letters*, Vol. 43, No. 23, (Nov. 2007), pp. (1260-1261).

Omeni, O.; Rodríguez-Villegas, E. & Toumazou, C. (2005). A Micropower CMOS Continuous-Time Filter With On-Chip Automatic Tuning, *IEEE Transactions on Circuits and Systems I*, Vol. 52, No. 4, (April 2005), pp. (695-705).

Ou, Hsin-Hung; Chen, Ya-Chi & Liu, Bin-Da (2006). A 0.7-V 10-bit 3 μW Analog-to-digital Converter for Implantable Biomedical Applications, *IEEE Biomedical Circuits and Systems Conference, BioCAS 2006*, (2006), pp. (122-125).

Ozgun, M. T.; Tsividis, Y. & Burra, G. (2006). Dynamic power optimization of active filters with application to zero-IF receivers, *IEEE Journal of Solid-State Circuits*. Vol. 41, No 6. (June 2006), pp. (1344-1352). ISSN 0018-9200.

Park, S.; Palaskas, Y. & Flynn, M.P. A 4-GS/s 4-bit Flash ADC in 0.18-μm CMOS. IEEE *Journal of Solid state circuits*, vol. 42, n°2, September 2007, pp. (1865-1872).

Pavan, S; Krishnapura, N.; Pandarinathan, R. & Sankar, P. (2008). A Power Optimized Continuous-Time SD ADC for Audio Applications. *IEEE Journal of Solid-State Circuits*, Vol. 43, No. 2, (Feb. 2008), pp.(351-360).

Pavan, S. and Sankar, P. (2010). *Power Reduction in Continuous-Time Delta-Sigma Modulators Using the Assisted Opamp Technique*. IEEE Journal of Solid-State Circuits, Vo. 45, No. 7, (July 2010), pp. (1365-1379).

Ramírez-Angulo, J. & Holmes, M. (2002). Simple technique using local CMFB to enhance slew rate and bandwidth of one-stage CMOS op-amps, *Electronics Letters*, Vol.38, No.23, (November 2002), pp. (1409- 1411). ISSN 0013-5194.

Ramírez-Angulo, J.; Urquidi, C. A.; González-Carvajal, R.; Torralba, A. & López-Martín, A. J. (2003). A new family of very low voltage analog circuits based on quasi-floating-gate transistors, *IEEE Transactions on Circuits and Systems II*, Vol. 50, No. 5, (May 2003), pp. (568–571).

Ramírez-Angulo, J.; López-Martín, A. J.; Carvajal, R. G. & Muñoz-Chavero, F. (2004). Very low-voltage analog signal processing based on quasi-floating gate transistors, *IEEE Journal of Solid-State Circuits*, Vol. 39, No. 3, (March 2004), pp. (434–442).

Ramírez-Angulo, J.; Carvajal, R. G.; Galan, J. & López-Martín, A. J. (2006). A free but efficient low-voltage class-AB two-stage operational amplifier, *IEEE Transactions on Circuits and Systems II*, Vol. 53, No. 7, (July 2006), pp. (214–220), ISSN 1549-7747.

Roh, J.; Byun, S.; Choi, Y.; Roh, H.; Kim, Y. & Kwon, J. (2008). A 0.9-V 60μW 1-Bit Fourth-Order Delta-Sigma Modulator With 83-dB Dynamic Range. *IEEE Journal of Solid-State Circuits*, Vol. 43, No. 2, (Feb. 2008), pp.(361-370).

Sánchez-Sinencio, E. & Silva-Martínez, J., (2000), CMOS transconductance amplifiers, architectures and active filters: a tutorial, *IEE Proceedings Circuits, Devices and Systems*. Vol. 147, No. 1, (February 2001), pp. (3-12). ISSN 1350-2409.

Sasidhar, N.; Y.-J. Kook; Takeuchi, S.; Hamashita, K.; Takasuka, K.;Hanumolu, P.K. & U.-K. Moon; A Low Power Pipelined ADC Using Capacitor and Opamp Sharing Technique With a Scheme to Cancel the Effect of Signal Dependent Kickback. *IEEE Journal of Solid-State Circuits*, vol.44, no.9, Sept. 2009, pp. (2392-2401)

Sawigun, C. & Serdijn, W.A. (2009). Ultra-low-power, class-AB, CMOS four-quadrant current multiplier, *Electronics Letters*. Vol.45, No.10, (May 2007), pp. (483-484). ISSN 0013-5194.

Sawigun, C.; Serdijn, W.A. (2011). Analysis and Design of a Low-Voltage, Low-Power, High-Precision, Class-AB Current-Mode Subthreshold CMOS Sample and Hold Circuit, *IEEE Transactions on Circuits and Systems I: Regular Papers*. Vol.58, No.7, (July 2011), pp.(1615-1626). ISSN 1549-8328.

Shahab, A. (December 2010). *On Achieving the Minimum Energy for Sending One Single Bit with Feedback*. MSc Thesis from Delft University of Technology. Available from: http://repository.tudelft.nl/.

Shin, S.-K.; You, Y.-S.; Lee, S.-H.; Moon, K.-H.; Kim, J.-W.; Brooks, L. and Lee, H. S. (2008). *A fully-differential zero-crossing-based 1.2 V 10b 26 MS/s pipelined ADC in 65 nm CMOS*, IEEE Trans. VLSI Syst., (Jun. 2008).

Steyaert, M.; Bijker, W. & Sevenhans, J. (1991). ECL-CMOS and CMOS-ECL interface in 1.2-pm CMOS for 1.50-MHz digital ECL data transmission systems, *IEEE Journal of Solid-State Circuits*, Vol. 26, No. 1, (January 1991), pp. (18–24).

Sundström, T. & Alvandpour, A. Utilizing process variations for reference generation in a Flash ADC. *IEEE transactions on circuits and systems II*, vol. 56, n° 5, May 2009, pp. (364-368).

Tan, C. & Chen, Z., An efficient CMOS operational amplifier for driving large capacitive loads, International Conference on ASIC, ASICON 2007, ISBN 978-1-4244-1132-0, Guilin, October 2007.

Tsividis, Y. (2002). *Mixed Analog-Digital VLSI Devices and Technology*. World Scientific, ISBN: 9812381112, Singapore.

Van der Plas, G.; Decoutere, S. & Donnay, S. A 0.16pJ/Conversion-Step 2.5mW 1.25 GS/s 4b ADC in a 90nm Digital CMOS Process. *Digest of Technical Papers of IEEE International Solid-State Circuits Conference 2006, February 2006*.

van Veldhoven, R. H. M. van; Rutten, R. and Breems, L. J. (2008). An inverter based hybrid $\Sigma\Delta$ modulator, IEEE Int. Solid-State Circuits Conf. Dig. Tech. Papers, (Feb. 2008), pp. (492–493).

Vaz, A.; Solar, H.; Rebollo, I.; Gutierrez, I. and Berenguer, R. (2010). *Long range, low power UHF RFID analog front-end suitable for batteryless wireless sensors*, IEEE International Microwave Symposium Digest, (May 2010), pp.(836-839).

Vittoz, E. A. (1994). Micropower techniques, In: *Design of MOS VLSI Circuits for Telecommunications*. Prentice-Hall, ISBN: 0-13-203639-8, USA.

Vittoz, E. A. (2009). Weak Inversion for Ultra Low-Power and Very Low-Voltage Circuits, *IEEE Asian Solid-State Circuits Conference*, (November 2009), pp. (129-132).

Wang, H.; Xu, J. and Wu, X. (2009). *A high power efficiency Class AB switched-opamp for low voltage low power sigma-delta modulators*. IEEE International Conference of Electron Devices and Solid-State Circuits, EDSSC 2009. Vol. , No., (25-27 Dec. 2009). pp.(429-432).

Wismar, U.; Wisland, D. & Andreani, P. (2006). A 0.2V 0.44µW 20 kHz Analog to Digital SD Modulator with 57 fJ/conversion FoM. *Proceedings of the 32nd European Solid-State Circuits Conference, 2006. ESSCIRC 2006*, (19-21 Sept. 2006), pp.(187-190).

Yang, H.Y.; Sarpeshkar, R. (2005). *A time-based energy-efficient analog-to-digital converter*, IEEE Journal of Solid-State Circuits, Vol.40, No.8, (Aug. 2005), pp.(1590- 1601).

Yang, H.Y.; Sarpeshkar, R. (2006). *A Bio-Inspired Ultra-Energy-Efficient Analog-to-Digital Converter for Biomedical Applications*. IEEE Transactions on Circuits and Systems I: Regular Papers, Vol.53, No.11, (Nov. 2006), pp.(2349-2356).

Yao, L.; Steyaert, M. S. J. & Sansen, W. (2004). A 1-V 140-lA 88-dB audio sigma-delta modulator in 90-nm CMOS, *IEEE Journal of Solid-State Circuits*, Vol. 39, No. 11, (November 2004), pp. (1809–1818).

Yao, L.; Steyaert, M. & Sansen, W. (2006). *Low-Power Low-Voltage Sigma-Delta Modulators in Nanometer CMOS*. Springer. ISBN-13 978-1-4020-4139-6 (HB), The Netherlands.

Yeknami, A.F.; Qazi, F.; Dabrowski; J.J. and Alvandpour, A. (2010). *Design of OTAs for Ultra-Low-Power Sigma-Delta ADCs in Medical Applications*. International Conference on Signals and Electronics Systems ICSES, Poland, September 2010.

3

Self-Cancellation of Sampling Frequency Offsets in STBC-OFDM Based Cooperative Transmissions

Zhen Gao[1] and Mary Ann Ingram[2]

[1]*Tsinghua University, Tsinghua Research Institute of Information Technology,*
Tsinghua National Laboratory for Information Science and Technology
[2]*Georgia Institute of Technology*
[1]*P.R. China*
[2]*USA*

1. Introduction

Orthogonal frequency division multiplexing (OFDM) is a popular modulation technique for wireless communications (Heiskala & Terry, 2002; Nee & Prasad, 2000). Because OFDM is very effective for combating multi-path fading with low complex channel estimation and equalization in the frequency domain, the OFDM-based cooperative transmission (CT) with distributed space-time coding becomes a very promising approach for achieving spatial diversity for the group of single-antenna equipped devices (Shin et al., 2007; Li & Xia, 2007; Zhang, 2008; Li et al., 2010). Duo to the spacial diversity gain, CT is an energy efficient transmission technique, which can be used in sensor networks, cellular networks, or even satellite networks, to improve the communication quality or coverage.

However, OFDM systems are sensitive to sampling frequency offset (SFO), which may lead to severe performance degradation (Pollet, 1994). In OFDM based CTs, because the oscillator for DAC on each relay is independent, multiple SFOs exist at the receiver, which is a very difficult problem to cope with (Kleider et al., 2009). The common used correction method for single SFO is interpolation/decimation (or named re-sampling), which is a energy consuming procedure. And what is more important is that, because the re-sampling of the received signal can only correct single SFO, it seems helpless to multiple SFOs in the case of OFDM based CTs. Although the estimation of multiple SFOs in OFDM-based CT systems has been addressed by several researchers (Kleider et al., 2009; Morelli et al., 2010), few contributions have addressed the correction of multiple SFOs in OFDM-based CT systems so far to our knowledge. One related work is the tracking problem in MIMO-OFDM systems (Oberli, 2007), but it is assumed that all transmitting branches are driven by a common sampling clock, so there is still only one SFO at the receiver.

To provide an energy efficient solution to the synchronization problem of SFOs in OFDM based CTs, in Section 2 of this chapter, we firstly introduce a low-cost self-cancellation scheme that we have proposed for single SFO in conventional OFDM systems. Then we will show in the Section 3 that, the combination of the self-cancellation for single SFO and the re-sampling method can solve the two SFOs problem in the two-branch STBC-OFDM based CTs. Simulations in the Section 4 will show that this low-cost scheme outperforms the ideal STBC system with no SFOs, and is robust to the mean SFO estimation error. In Section 5, the energy efficiency problem of the proposed schemes is analyzed. The chapter is summarized in Section 6.

2. SFO self-cancellation for conventional OFDM systems

The effect of SFO on the performance of OFDM systems was first addressed by T. Pollet (Pollet, 1994). SFO mainly introduces two problems in the frequency domain: inter-channel interference (ICI) and phase rotation of constellations. As mentioned in (Pollet, 1994; Speth et al., 1999; Pollet & Peeters, 1999; Kai et al., 2005) the power of the ICI is so small that the ICI are usually taken as additional noise. So the removal of SFO is mainly the correction of phase rotation.

Three methods have been proposed to correct single SFO. The first is to control the sampling frequency of the ADC directly at the receiver (Pollet & Peeters, 1999; Kim et al., 1998; Simoens et al., 2000). However, according to (Horlin & Bourdoux, 2008), this method does not suitable for low-cost analog front-ends. The second method is interpolation/ decimation (Speth et al., 1999; Kai et al. 2005; Speth et al., 2001; Fechtel, 2000; Sliskovic, 2001; Shafiee et al. 2004). The SFO is corrected by re-sampling the base-band signal in the time domain. The problem of this method is that the complexity is so high that it's very energy consuming for high-speed broadband applications. The third method is to rotate the constellations in the frequency domain (Pollet & Peeters, 1999; Kim et al. 1998;). The basis for this method is the delay-rotor property (Pollet & Peeters, 1999), which is that the SFO in the time domain causes phase shifts that are linearly proportional to the subcarrier index in the frequency domain. The performance of such method relies on the accuracy of SFO estimation. In previous works, there are three methods for SFO estimation. The first method is cyclic prefix (CP)-based estimation (Heaton, 2001). The performance of this method relies on the length of CP and the delay spread of the multipath channel. The second is the pilot-based method (Kim et al. 1998; Speth et al., 2001; Fechtel, 2000; Liu & Chong, 2002). The problem with this method is that, because the pilots are just a small portion of the symbol, it always takes several ten's of OFDM symbols for the tracking loop to converge. The third is the decision-directed (DD) method (Speth et al., 1999; Simoens et al., 2000). The problem of this method is that when SFO is large, the hard decisions are not reliable, so the decisions need to be obtained by decoding and re-constructing the symbol, which requires more memory and higher complexity. Because no estimation method is perfect, the correction method relying on the estimation will not be perfect.

Based on above considerations, we proposed a low-cost SFO self-cancellation scheme for conventional OFDM systems in (Gao & Ingram, 2010). In this section, we give a brief introduction of the self-cancellation scheme for single SFO, and then Section 3 will show how this scheme can be applied for the problem of two SFOs in STBC-OFDM based CTs.

Instead of focusing on the linearity between phase shifts caused by SFO and subcarrier index as usual, the scheme in (Gao & Ingram, 2010) makes use of the symmetry property of the phase shifts. By putting the same constellation on symmetrical subcarrier pairs, and combining the pair coherently at the receiver, the phase shifts caused by SFO on symmetrical subcarriers approximately cancel each other. Considering that the residual CFO may exist in the signal, pilots are also inserted symmetrically in each OFDM symbol, so that the phase tracking for residual CFO can work as usual. Although it can be expected that, because no SFO estimation and correction processing are needed, the complexity and energy consuming of the SFO self-cancellation should be very low, this aspect is not considered carefully in (Gao & Ingram, 2010). So in this chapter, a detailed discussion about the complexity problem for the proposed scheme is provided in Section 5.

2.1 Signal model

The FFT length (or number of subcarriers) is N, in which N_d subcarriers are used for data symbols and N_p subcarriers are used for pilot symbols. The length of CP is N_g, so the total length of one OFDM symbol is $N_s = N + N_g$. f_s denotes the sampling frequency of the receiver, and $T_s = 1/f_s$ is the sample duration at the receiver. We assume the symbol on the k-th subcarrier is a_k, H_k is the channel response on the k-th subcarrier, Δf is the residual CFO normalized by the subcarrier spacing, and $\varepsilon = (T_{s\text{-}tx} - T_s)/T_s$ is the SFO, where $T_{s\text{-}tx}$ is the sample duration at the transmitter. Then the transmitted signal in the time domain can be expressed as

$$x_n = \frac{1}{N} \sum_{k=-N/2}^{N/2-1} a_k e^{j2\pi nk/N}, \; n = 0,1,...N-1. \tag{1}$$

After passing through the physical channel h_l and corrupted by the residual CFO Δf and SFO ε, the complex envelope of the received signal without noise can be expressed as

$$\begin{aligned} r_n &= e^{j2\pi\Delta fn/N}\left(h_l * x_n\right) \\ &= e^{j2\pi\Delta fn/N}\frac{1}{N}\sum_{k=-N/2}^{N/2-1} a_k H_k e^{j2\pi n(1+\varepsilon)k/N} \end{aligned} \cdot \tag{2}$$

After removing the CP and performing DFT to r_n, the symbol in the frequency domain can be expressed as (Zhao & Haggman, 2001)

$$\begin{aligned} z_k &= \sum_{n=0}^{N-1} r_n e^{-j2\pi kn/N} \\ &= \sum_{n=0}^{N-1}\left[e^{j2\pi\Delta fn/N}\frac{1}{N}\sum_{k=-N/2}^{N/2-1} X_k H_k e^{j2\pi n(1+\varepsilon)k/N}\right] e^{-j2\pi kn/N}, \\ &= a_k H_k S(\Delta f + \varepsilon k) + \sum_{\substack{l=-N/2 \\ l\neq k}}^{N/2-1} a_l H_l S(\Delta f + \varepsilon l + l - k) \end{aligned} \tag{3}$$

where $S(x) = \dfrac{\sin[\pi x]}{N\sin[\pi x/N]} e^{j\pi x(N_s+N_g-1)/N}$.

Now, if the constellation transmitted on the k-th subcarrier of the m-th OFDM symbol and the corresponding noise are $a_{m,k}$ and $w_{m,k}$, respectively, the received symbol in the frequency domain can be easily got from (3) as

$$z_{m,k} = (e^{j\pi\phi_k} e^{j2\pi((mN_s+N_g)/N)\phi_k}) \text{sinc}(\pi\phi_k) a_{m,k} H_k + w_{ICI,k} + w_{m,k} , \qquad (4)$$

where $\phi_k \approx \Delta f + \varepsilon k$, $\text{sinc}(\pi\phi_k) = \dfrac{\sin \pi\phi_k}{N \sin(\pi\phi_k/N)}$ and $w_{ICI,k} = \displaystyle\sum_{\substack{l=-N/2 \\ l \neq k}}^{N/2-1} a_l H_l S(\Delta f + \varepsilon l + l - k)$ is the

ICIs from all other subcarriers.

In (4), $e^{j\pi\phi_k}$ and $\text{sinc}(\pi\phi_k)$ are the local phase increment and local amplitude gain, respectively. They will be combined into the estimated channel response as $H_k' = e^{j\pi\phi_k} \text{sinc}(\pi\phi_k) H_k$. So, after channel equalization, (4) becomes

$$z_{m,k} = e^{j2\pi((mN_s+N_g)/N)\phi_k} a_{m,k} + w'_{ICI,k} + w'_{m,k} , \qquad (5)$$

where $w'_{ICI,k} = w_{ICI,k} / H_k'$ and $w'_{m,k} = w_{m,k} / H_k'$. In (5), only the accumulated phase $e^{j2\pi((mN_s+N_g)/N)\phi_k}$ needs to be corrected.

2.2 The idea of SFO self-cancellation scheme

The SFO self-cancellation scheme is inspired by the relationship between phase shifts and the subcarrier index. Fig. 1 is a simulation result that demonstrates the phase shifts caused

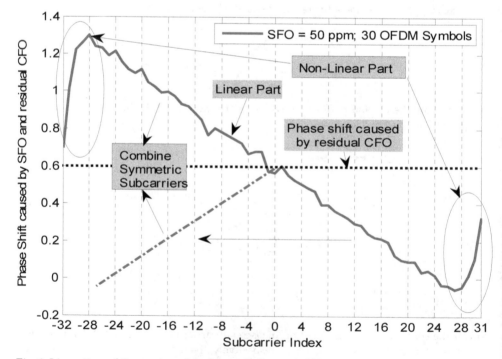

Fig. 1. Linearity and Symmetry of the Phase Shifts caused by SFO

by residual CFO and SFO. The figure shows two phenomenons. The first is that the phase shifts for the subcarriers in the middle are linearly proportional to the subcarrier index. This is the delay-rotor property mentioned above, and has been explored a lot for estimation and correction of SFO. Note that the phase shifts for the edge subcarriers do not obey the linearity. In practice, for the convenience of design of transmit and receive filters, and inter-channel interference suppression, these subcarriers are usually set to be zeros (IEEE, 1999). The other fact is that the phase shifts caused by SFO are symmetrical relative to the common phase shift caused by residual CFO (dotted horizontal line in Fig. 1). So if we put the same constellation on symmetrical subcarriers, we may be able to combine the symbols at the receiver in a way such that the phase shifts on these two subcarriers caused by SFO can approximately cancel each other. This mapping can be called "Symmetric Symbol Repetition (SSR)", which is different from other self-cancellation techniques, such as "Adjacent Symbol Repetition (ASR)" (Zhao & Haggman, 2001), "Adjacent Conjugate Symbol Repetition (ACSR)" (Sathananthan, 2004), and "Symmetric Conjugate Symbol Repetition (SCSR)" (Tang, 2007). It should be pointed out that the self-cancellation of the phase shifts caused by SFO on symmetric subcarrier cannot be achieved by other repetition schemes. Taking SCSR as an example, the addition of conjugate symbols on symmetric subcarriers also removes the phase of the symbols, which makes the symbol undetectable.

2.3 Analysis of the SFO self-cancellation scheme

Assuming the same constellation $a_{m,k}$ is mapped on symmetrical subcarriers $-k$ and k of the m-th OFDM symbol, the signal on the pair of subcarriers after channel equalization can be expressed as (according to (5))

$$\begin{cases} z_{m,k} = e^{jF_m\phi_k} a_{m,k} + w'_{ICI,k} + w'_{m,k} \\ z_{m,-k} = e^{jF_m\phi_{-k}} a_{m,k} + w'_{ICI,-k} + w'_{m,-k} \end{cases}, \tag{6}$$

where $F_m = 2\pi((mN_s + N_g)/N)$. Then the combination of $z_{m,k}$ and $z_{m,-k}$ is

$$z'_{m,k} = 2\cos(F_m\varepsilon k)e^{jF_m\Delta f} a_{m,k} + \alpha w'_{ICI,k} + w''_{m,k}. \tag{7}$$

We see that the phase shifts introduced by SFO is removed, and the residual phase $e^{jF_m\Delta f}$ is a common term, which can be corrected by phase tracking. Because $F_m\varepsilon k \ll 1$, $2\cos(F_m\varepsilon k) \approx 2$. In other words, the two subcarriers are combined coherently. In addition, because the energy of ICIs is mainly from residual CFO, and the ICIs caused by residual CFO are same for symmetrical subcarriers, the ICIs on symmetrical subcarriers are also combined almost coherently, which means $a \approx 2$. So the average SIR does not change after combination. $w'_{m,k}$ and $w'_{m,-k}$ are independent, so the final noise term is

$$w''_{m,k} = w'_{m,k} + w'_{m,-k} = w_{m,k}/H_k' + w_{m,-k}/H_{-k}'. \tag{8}$$

Assuming $E\{|a_{m,k}|^2\} = 1$, $E\{|H_k|^2\} = 1$, $E\{|w_{ICI,k}|^2\} = \sigma_{ICI}^2$, and $E\{|w_{m,k}|^2\} = \sigma_n^2$, under the assumption that $\sigma_{ICI}^2 \ll \sigma_n^2$, the average SINR before combination (see (5)) and after combination (see (7)) are

$$\begin{cases} SINR_{Bf} = \dfrac{1}{\sigma_{ICI}{}^2 + \sigma_n{}^2} \approx \dfrac{1}{\sigma_n{}^2} \\[4mm] SINR_{Af} \approx \dfrac{4}{4\sigma_{ICI}{}^2 + 2\sigma_n{}^2} \approx \dfrac{2}{\sigma_n{}^2} \end{cases} \tag{9}$$

So the average SINR has been improved by 3dB, which is the array gain from the combination. In addition, because small values are more likely to get for $2|H_k'|^2$ than for $(1/|H_k'|^2 + 1/|H_{-k}'|^2)^{-1}$, some diversity gain is achieved. Fig. 2 shows that this diversity gain is smaller that of the 2-branch MRC. In the figure, H1, H2 and H are independent Rayleigh fading random variables.

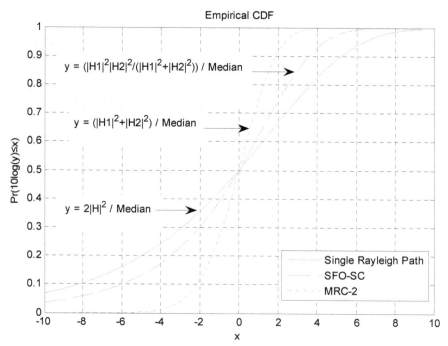

Fig. 2. Diversity gain from Symmetric Combination

2.4 System structure

Fig. 3 gives the structure of the transmitter and receiver with the SFO self-cancellation scheme. At the transmitter, the "Modulation on Half Subcarriers" and "Symmetrical Mapping" blocks compose the "Self-Cancellation Encoding" module. At the receiver, the "Channel Equalization" and "Symmetrical Combining" blocks compose the "Self-Cancellation Decoding" module. For the coarse CFO synchronization and channel estimation, repeated short training blocks and repeated long training blocks compose the preamble. To remove the residual CFO, the phase shifts on pilots after the SFO self-cancellation decoding are averaged to get one phase shift, which is multiplied to all the data subcarriers after the self-cancellation decoding.

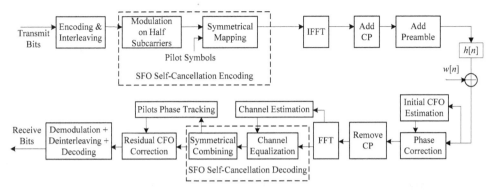

Fig. 3. Block diagram of the Transmitter and Receiver with the SFO Self-Cancellation Scheme

Fig. 4 shows how to do the symmetrical mapping. For the purpose of phase tracking for residual CFO correction, pilot symbols are also mapped symmetrically. For the convenient of design of transmit filter and receive filter, the subcarriers on the edge are set to be zeros.

Fig. 4. Symmetrical Mapping

3. SFOs self-cancellation scheme for Alamouti coded OFDM based CTs

In this section, we propose a self-cancellation scheme for the two SFOs in the 2-branch Alamouti coded OFDM based CT systems. The scheme is the combination of the SFO self-cancellation scheme introduced in Section 2 and the re-sampling method, which is the conventional method for single SFO compensation.

3.1 Alamouti coded OFDM based cooperative transmission

We consider a commonly used cooperative system model (Fig. 5), which includes one source, one relay and one destination. Every node is equipped with one antenna. This structure is a very popular choice for coverage increase in sensor networks and for quality improvement for uplink transmissions in cellular networks (Shin et al., 2007). The communication includes two phases. In Phase 1, the source broadcasts the message to the relay and the destination. We assume the relay can decode the message correctly. Then, both the relay and the source will do 2-branch STBC-OFDM encoding according to Alamouti scheme (Alamouti, 1998). In Phase 2, the source transmits one column of the STBC matrix to the destination, and the relay transmits the other column. In Fig. 5, (f_1, T_1), (f_2, T_2), (f_d, T_d) are the carrier frequency and sample duration of the source, relay and the destination, respectively. This structure is well studied by (Shin, 2007). In this section, we assume timing synchronization and coarse carrier frequency synchronization have been performed according to (Shin, 2007), so only residual CFOs and SFOs exist in the received signal at the destination.

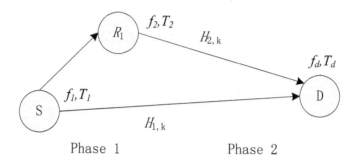

Fig. 5. Cooperative Transmission Architecture

3.2 Effect of residual CFOs and SFOs in Alamouti coded signals

According to the Alamouti scheme (Alamouti, 1998), the transmitted signal matrix for the k-th subcarrier by the source and the relay in two successive OFDM symbols is

$$\begin{bmatrix} a_{m,k} & -a_{m+1,k}^{*} \\ a_{m+1,k} & a_{m,k}^{*} \end{bmatrix}.$$

The first column is for the m-th OFDM symbol duration and the second column is for the $(m+1)$-th OFDM symbol duration. If there are no CFOs and SFOs, the received signals on the k-th subcarrier of successive OFDM symbols are

$$\begin{cases} z_{m,k} = a_{m,k}H_{1,k} + a_{m+1,k}H_{2,k} + w_{m,k} \\ z_{m+1,k} = -a_{m+1,k}^{*}H_{1,k} + a_{m,k}^{*}H_{2,k} + w_{m,k+1} \end{cases}, \tag{10}$$

where $H_{t,k}$ ($t = 1, 2$) is the frequency domain response of the channels between two transmitters and the destination. We assume the channels are static during the transmission of one packet.

If the residual CFOs and SFOs between the two transmitters and the destination are $(\Delta f_1, \varepsilon_1)$ and $(\Delta f_2, \varepsilon_2)$, following the procedure in Section 2.1, the received OFDM symbols at the destination become

$$z_{m,k} = a_{m,k}e^{j\pi\phi_{1,k}}e^{jF_m\phi_{1,k}}\mathrm{sinc}(\phi_{1,k})H_{1,k} + a_{m+1,k}e^{j\pi\phi_{2,k}}e^{jF_m\phi_{2,k}}\mathrm{sinc}(\phi_{2,k})H_{2,k} \\ + w_{m,ICI} + w_{m,k} \tag{11}$$

and

$$z_{m+1,k} = -a_{m+1,k}^{*}e^{j\pi\phi_{1,k}}e^{jF_{m+1}\phi_{1,k}}\mathrm{sinc}(\phi_{1,k})H_{1,k} + a_{m,k}^{*}e^{j\pi\phi_{2,k}}e^{jF_{m+1}\phi_{2,k}}\mathrm{sinc}(\phi_{2,k})H_{2,k} \\ + w_{m+1,ICI} + w_{m+1,k} \tag{12}$$

in which $\phi_{t,k} = \Delta f_t + \varepsilon_t k$, and $w_{m,ICI}$ and $w_{m+1,ICI}$ are the ICIs caused by residual CFOs and SFOs. Because the power of ICI is very small, $w_{m,ICI}$ and $w_{m+1,ICI}$ are usually taken as additional noise. So we can define $w'_{m,k} = w_{m,ICI} + w_{m,k}$ and $w'_{m+1,k} = w_{m+1,ICI} + w_{m+1,k}$ as the effective noise.

In (11) and (12), $e^{j\pi\phi_{t,k}}$ and $\text{sinc}(\pi\phi_{t,k})$ are the local phase increment and local amplitude attenuation caused by the residual CFOs and SFOs, respectively, and they are usually combined into the estimated channel responses as $H'_{t,k} = e^{j\pi\phi_{t,k}}\text{sinc}(\pi\phi_{t,k})H_{t,k}$. Before STBC decoding, these two estimated channels are corrected through phase tracking based on pilot symbols (Shin, 2007). In this section, we assume the channel estimations and phase tracking for residual CFOs are perfect, so that we can focus on the effect of SFOs. If $\varphi_t = F_m\Delta f_t$ and $\theta_{t,k} = F_m\varepsilon_t k$, the channel responses after phase correction becomes $H''_{t,k} = e^{j\pi\varphi_t}e^{j\pi\phi_{t,k}}\text{sinc}(\pi\phi_{t,k})H_{t,k}$. Then the STBC decoded symbols are

$$
\begin{aligned}
\hat{a}_{m,k} &= (H''_{1,k}{}^* z_{m,k} + H''_{2,k} z_{m+1,k}{}^*)/\left(\left|H''_{1,k}\right|^2 + \left|H''_{2,k}\right|^2\right) \\
&= \frac{\left(a_{m,k}e^{j\theta_{1,k}}\left|H''_{1,k}\right|^2 + a_{m,k}e^{-j\theta_{2,k}}\left|H''_{2,k}\right|^2 + a_{m+1,k}e^{j\theta_{2,k}}H''_{2,k}H''_{1,k}{}^* - a_{m+1,k}e^{-j\theta_{1,k}}H''_{2,k}H''_{1,k}{}^*\right)}{\left(\left|H''_{1,k}\right|^2 + \left|H''_{2,k}\right|^2\right)} \\
&\quad + \left(H''_{1,k}{}^* w'_{m,k} + H''_{2,k} w'_{m+1,k}{}^*\right)/\left(\left|H''_{1,k}\right|^2 + \left|H''_{2,k}\right|^2\right)
\end{aligned}
\tag{13}
$$

and

$$
\begin{aligned}
\hat{a}_{m+1,k} &= (H''_{2,k}{}^* z_{m,k} - H''_{1,k} z_{m+1,k}{}^*)/\left(\left|H''_{1,k}\right|^2 + \left|H''_{2,k}\right|^2\right) \\
&\approx \frac{\left(a_{m+1,k}e^{j\theta_{2,k}}\left|H''_{2,k}\right|^2 + a_{m+1,k}e^{-j\theta_{1,k}}\left|H''_{1,k}\right|^2 + a_{m,k}e^{j\theta_{1,k}}H''_{2,k}{}^* H''_{1,k} - a_{m,k}e^{-j\theta_{2,k}}H''_{2,k}{}^* H''_{1,k}\right)}{\left(\left|H''_{1,k}\right|^2 + \left|H''_{2,k}\right|^2\right)} \\
&\quad + (H''_{1,k}{}^* w'_{m,k} - H''_{2,k} w'_{m+1,k}{}^*)/\left(\left|H''_{1,k}\right|^2 + \left|H''_{2,k}\right|^2\right)
\end{aligned}
\tag{14}
$$

where we apply the approximation $F_m \approx F_{m+1}$ in (14). From (13) and (14) we see that, the SFOs destroy the orthogonality of the two STBC branches, so the symbols cannot be recovered perfectly by STBC decoding.

3.3 SFOs self-cancellation

If we apply the SFO self-cancellation scheme for single SFO directly into STBC decoded signals, the symbol on the k-th subcarrier after symmetrical combination becomes

$$
\begin{aligned}
\hat{a}'_{m,k} &= \hat{a}_{m,k} + \hat{a}_{m,-k} \\
&= \frac{a_{m,k}e^{j\theta_{1,k}}\left|H''_{1,k}\right|^2 + a_{m,k}e^{-j\theta_{2,k}}\left|H''_{2,k}\right|^2}{\left|H''_{1,k}\right|^2 + \left|H''_{2,k}\right|^2} + \frac{a_{m,k}e^{-j\theta_{1,k}}\left|H''_{1,-k}\right|^2 + a_{m,k}e^{j\theta_{2,k}}\left|H''_{2,-k}\right|^2}{\left|H''_{1,-k}\right|^2 + \left|H''_{2,-k}\right|^2} \\
&\quad + \frac{a_{m+1,k}e^{j\theta_{2,k}}H''_{2,k}H''_{1,k}{}^* - a_{m+1,k}e^{-j\theta_{1,k}}H''_{2,k}H''_{1,k}{}^*}{\left|H''_{1,k}\right|^2 + \left|H''_{2,k}\right|^2} + \frac{a_{m+1,k}e^{-j\theta_{2,k}}H''_{2,-k}H''_{1,-k}{}^* - a_{m+1,-k}e^{j\theta_{1,k}}H''_{2,-k}H''_{1,-k}{}^*}{\left|H''_{1,-k}\right|^2 + \left|H''_{2,-k}\right|^2} \\
&\quad + \frac{H''_{1,k}{}^* w'_{m,k} + H''_{2,k} w'_{m+1,k}{}^*}{\left|H''_{1,k}\right|^2 + \left|H''_{2,k}\right|^2} + \frac{H''_{1,-k}{}^* w'_{m,-k} + H''_{2,-k} w'_{m+1,-k}{}^*}{\left|H''_{1,-k}\right|^2 + \left|H''_{2,-k}\right|^2}
\end{aligned}
\tag{15}
$$

By examining the structure of (15) carefully, we find that if $\theta_{1,k} = -\theta_{2,k} = \theta_k$, or equivalently $\varepsilon_1 = -\varepsilon_2 = \varepsilon$, the interference term (the second line of (15)) becomes zero, and then we can have

$$\hat{a}'_{m,k} = G_{m,k}a_{m,k} + w''_{m,k} , \qquad (16)$$

where we define

$$G_{m,k} = 2\cos(F_m\varepsilon k) \text{ and } w''_{m,k} = \frac{H''^{*}_{1,k}w'_{m,k} + H''_{2,k}w'^{*}_{m+1,k}}{\left|H''_{1,k}\right|^2 + \left|H''_{2,k}\right|^2} + \frac{H''^{*}_{1,-k}w'_{m,-k} + H''_{2,-k}w'^{*}_{m+1,-k}}{\left|H''_{1,-k}\right|^2 + \left|H''_{2,-k}\right|^2} .$$

From (16), we see that if we can make $\varepsilon_1 = -\varepsilon_2 = \varepsilon$, the phase shifts and interferences caused by SFOs can be completely removed, and the symbols can be detected successively. Fortunately, interpolation/decimation, or re-sampling, can help us to achieve this goal. Firstly, the receiver need to estimate the mean value of the two SFOs, and then adjust sampling frequency to the average of the two transmit sampling frequencies through re-sampling, which makes the two residual SFOs opposite. The discussion about the mean SFO estimation is given in Section 3.5, and simulations in Section 4 will show the robustness of our design to the mean SFO estimation error.

Fig. 6 describes a complete system structure with the SFOs self-cancellation scheme for Alamouti coded OFDM based CT. During the cooperation phase, SSR and Alamouti encoding are performed at the source and the relay. Then, the source transmits one column of the STBC matrix to the destination, and the relay transmits the other one. The preamble at the beginning of the packet includes the training for timing synchronization, initial CFO estimation, channel estimation, and mean SFO estimation. The estimated mean SFO is then used to adjust the sampling frequency through interpolation/decimation. This adjustment makes the residual SFOs in two branches opposite, which makes the STBC decoded symbols have the form of (16). Finally, the SFO self-cancellation decoding performs symmetrical combination to remove the effect of SFO in each orthogonal branch.

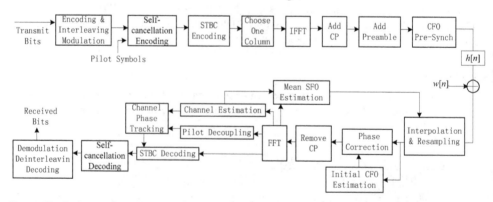

Fig. 6. Block diagram of the Self-Cancellation Scheme in Alamouti Coded OFDM based CTs

3.4 Analysis of diversity gain and array gain

Based on (16), the SNR after the SFO self-cancellation decoding can be calculated as

$$\frac{S_{stbc\text{-}sc}}{N_{stbc\text{-}sc}} = \frac{G_{m,k}^{2}\rho}{\sigma_{w}^{2}}\left(\frac{1}{\left|H_{1,k}''\right|^{2}+\left|H_{2,k}''\right|^{2}} + \frac{1}{\left|H_{1,-k}''\right|^{2}+\left|H_{2,-k}''\right|^{2}}\right)^{-1}.$$

So the SNR gain can be expressed as

$$G_{snr} = \frac{S_{stbc\text{-}sc}}{N_{stbc\text{-}sc}}\bigg/\frac{\rho}{\sigma_{w}^{2}} = G_{a}G_{d},$$

where we define

$$G_{a} = \frac{G_{m,k}^{2}}{2} \text{ and } G_{d} = 2\left(\frac{1}{\left|H_{1,k}''\right|^{2}+\left|H_{2,k}''\right|^{2}} + \frac{1}{\left|H_{1,-k}''\right|^{2}+\left|H_{2,-k}''\right|^{2}}\right)^{-1}$$

as the array gain and diversity gain, respectively. Because $F_{m}\varepsilon k \ll 1$, the array gain is a little bit smaller than 2. This gain comes from the fact that we combine the useful signals coherently, but the noise terms are added non-coherently. Fig. 7 plots G_{d} together with the CDF of standard Rayleigh and MRC of two Rayleigh random variables for normal STBC. We see that, in addition to the diversity gain from STBC, we get extra diversity gain from

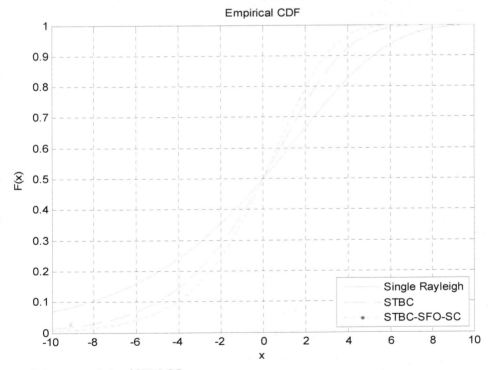

Fig. 7. Diversity Gain of STBC-SC

the SFO self-cancellation scheme. This is because the symmetrical combination actually averages the channels on symmetrical subcarriers, which makes the equivalent channel "flatter".

3.5 Discussion about the mean SFO estimation

There are two choices for the mean SFO estimation. One is to estimate the mean SFO directly, and the other is to estimate two SFOs separately and then get the mean value of the estimates. For direct estimation, two relays may transmit common training blocks, and the receiver does the SFO estimation based on the training using conventional SFO estimation method for single SFO. In this case, estimation result should be some kind of weighted average of the two SFOs, not exact the mean SFO. The second choice should be unbiased, but special training structure needs to be designed for the separate estimation. As mentioned in (Morelli, 2010), for the ML estimator of residual CFO and SFO, the two parameters are coupled, so the ML solution involves a 2-dimensional grid-search, which is difficult to pursue in practice. On the other hand, if we still need to estimate the two SFOs accurately, the self-cancellation scheme is not so valuable. So our comment is that, in the CT systems applying our SFOs self-cancellation schemes, the simple direct estimation of the mean SFO is favorable. Although the accuracy of this method may not be very high, the simulations in Section 4 will show that the self-cancellation scheme is robust to the estimation error. In addition, similar to the single SFO estimation for conventional OFDM systems, a PI (proportional-integral) tracking loop can be used to improve the accuracy of the mean SFO estimation (Speth et al., 2001).

4. Simulations

Simulations are run to examine the performance of our SFOs self-cancellation scheme in the STBC-OFDM based cooperative transmissions. In the simulation, $N = 64$, $N_g = 16$, $N_s = 80$, and one packet contains 50 OFDM symbols. No channel coding is applied in the simulations. The typical urban channel model COST207 (Commission of the European Communities, 1989) is used, and the channel power is normalized to be unity. We assume the difference between two SFOs is 100 ppm. If the mean SFO estimation is perfect, the residual SFO should be SFO1/SFO2 = 50/-50ppm. Because the mean SFO estimation may not be perfect, the phase shifts and interferences may still exist in the decoded signals. In following simulations, we firstly examine the effect of the mean SFO estimation error to the residual phase shifts and signal to interference radio (SIR) in both normal STBC and STBC with SFO self-cancellation (STBC-SC). And then we show the overall effect of SFOs to the constellations. Finally, we compare the BER performance of STBC and STBC-SC when two SFOs exist.

4.1 Residual phase shifts

Fig. 8 shows the residual phase after STBC decoding and SFO self-cancellation decoding for different SFO1/SFO2. For STBC, the residual phase is measured as $E\left[\angle \hat{a}_{m,k} a_{m,k}^* \right]$ (see (13)), and for STBC-SC, it is measured as $E\left[\angle \hat{a}'_{m,k} a_{m,k}^* \right]$ (see (15)). In the simulation, the value of SFO1 changes gradually from 0 to 100 ppm, and SFO2 changes correspondingly as SFO1 − 100 (ppm). Because the phase shifts are different for different subcarriers in different OFDM symbols, the 13th (k=13) and 26th (k=26) subcarriers in the 50th OFDM symbol (m = 50) are chosen as examples. Fig. 8 shows that the residual phase is reduced significantly by the symmetrical combination. The residual phase for STBC (circle lines) is only determined by the difference of the two SFOs (100ppm), and not very related to the value of SFO1 and SFO2. But for SFO self-cancellation (dot lines), when SFO1 = -SFO2, the residual phase is 0, and the larger is the mean SFO estimation error, the larger is the residual phase. For the 13th subcarrier, the increase of the residual phase is very small, so we can say the residual phase of STBC-SC is not sensitive to the mean SFO estimation error on average.

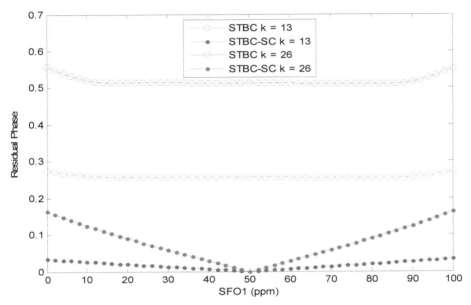

Fig. 8. Residual Phase (k=13/26, m=50)

4.2 SIR

When SFO1 ≠ -SFO2, interferences come out in the decoded symbols, and destroy the orthogonality of the STBC structure. Fig. 9 shows the SIR for STBC and STBC-SC for different SFO1/ SFO2. Based on (13) and (15), the SIR for STBC and STBC-SC are calculated as

$$
\begin{cases}
SIR_{stbc} = \dfrac{E\left[\left|a_{m,k}e^{j\theta_{1,k}}\left|H''_{1,k}\right|^2 + a_{m,k}e^{-j\theta_{2,k}}\left|H''_{2,k}\right|^2\right|^2\right]}{E\left[\left|a_{m+1,k}e^{j\theta_{2,k}}H''_{2,k}H''_{1,k}{}^* - a_{m+1,k}e^{-j\theta_{1,k}}H''_{2,k}H''_{1,k}{}^*\right|^2\right]} \\[4ex]
SIR_{stbc-sc} = \dfrac{E\left[\left|\dfrac{a_{m,k}e^{j\theta_{1,k}}\left|H''_{1,k}\right|^2 + a_{m,k}e^{-j\theta_{2,k}}\left|H''_{2,k}\right|^2}{\left|H''_{1,k}\right|^2 + \left|H''_{2,k}\right|^2} + \dfrac{a_{m,k}e^{-j\theta_{1,k}}\left|H''_{1,-k}\right|^2 + a_{m,k}e^{j\theta_{2,k}}\left|H''_{2,-k}\right|^2}{\left|H''_{1,-k}\right|^2 + \left|H''_{2,-k}\right|^2}\right|^2\right]}{E\left[\left|\dfrac{a_{m+1,k}e^{j\theta_{2,k}}H''_{2,k}H''_{1,k}{}^* - a_{m+1,k}e^{-j\theta_{1,k}}H''_{2,k}H''_{1,k}{}^*}{\left|H''_{1,k}\right|^2 + \left|H''_{2,k}\right|^2} + \dfrac{a_{m+1,k}e^{-j\theta_{2,k}}H''_{2,-k}H''_{1,-k}{}^* - a_{m+1,-k}e^{j\theta_{1,k}}H''_{2,-k}H''_{1,-k}{}^*}{\left|H''_{1,-k}\right|^2 + \left|H''_{2,-k}\right|^2}\right|^2\right]}
\end{cases}
$$

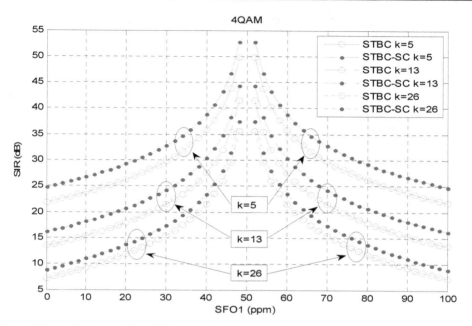

Fig. 9. SIR for Different SFO1/SFO2 (k=5/13/26, m=50)

We choose $k = 5/13/26$ and $m = 50$. We see that, for both STBC and STBC-SC, the larger is the mean SFO estimation error, the lower is the SIR. From (15), we can see that, in the symmetrical combination, useful signals are combined coherently, and the interferences are combined non-coherently. So the SIR for STBC-SC is about 3dB larger than that for STBC. When k is large, because the amplitude gain for STBC-SC, $G_{m,k}$ in equation (16), is obviously smaller than 2, the SIR improvement is smaller than 3dB (e.g. about 2dB for $k = 26$). Fig. 10 shows the SIR for the positive half part of the subcarriers when the mean SFO estimation is 20ppm (SFO1/SFO2 = 70/-30ppm). It's clear that the closer is the subcarrier to the center ($k = 0$), the larger is the SIR. Also, for small k, the improvement of SFO self-cancellation is about 3dB over STBC, but this improvement decreases for larger k.

4.3 Effect of SFOs to the constellations

Fig. 11 shows the effect of the SFOs to the decoded symbols in one packet for STBC and STBC-SC. No noise is added in the simulation. When there is no mean SFO estimation error (SFO1/SFO2 = 50/-50ppm, Fig. 11 (a)), there is no interference, so the effect of SFOs to STBC decoded symbols is just spreading one constellation point to a "strip", which effect is removed by the symmetrical combination in STBC-SC. When the mean SFO estimation error is 20ppm (SFO1/SFO2 = 70/-30ppm, Fig. 11 (b)), for STBC, the interferences are obvious for the points at the edges of the "phase spread strip", and much less obvious for the points in the middle of the strip. The reason is that, the points at the edges of the strip correspond to the symbols on the edge (e.g. k = ±25 or ±26). From Fig. 10 we know that the SIRs for these subcarriers are low, so the interferences are obvious. For STBC-SC, because the phase spread is mitigated, the influence range of the interferences is much smaller than that for STBC.

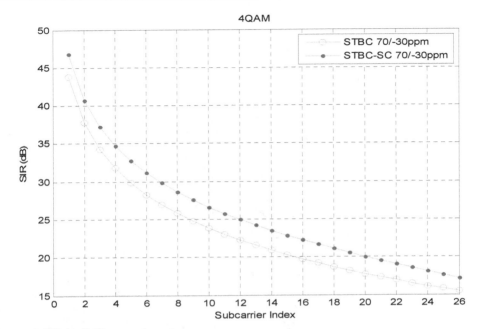

Fig. 10. SIR for Different subcarriers

4.4 BER performance

Fig. 12 shows the effect of SFOs to the BER performance of STBC and STBC-SC when QPSK is used. When SFO1/SFO2 = 50/-50ppm, STBC-SC outperforms STBC by about 5dB. When the mean SFO estimation error is 20ppm (SFO1/SFO2 = 70/-30ppm), the degradation of STBC for BER = 4×10^{-5} is more than 3dB, but the degradation of STBC-SC is less than 1dB. So we can say STBC-SC is robust to the mean SFO estimation error. The BER for STBC with no SFOs is also given as a reference (the triangle-dashed curve). We see that STBC-SC outperforms the ideal STBC by about 4dB when BER = 10^{-4}. Part of the improvement comes from the array gain and diversity gain brought by the symmetrical combination. But the more important reason is that, as shown in Fig. 11, STBC-SC decreases the phase shifts caused by SFOs significantly, which limits the influence range of the interferences.

Fig. 13 shows the BER performance of STBC and STBC-SC when SFO1/SFO2 = 50/-50ppm and SFO1/SFO2 = 70/-30ppm for 16QAM. We see that the STBC cannot work even for SFO1/SFO2 = 50/-50ppm. This is because the distances between constellations are closer than those for QPSK, the spreads of the constellation points caused by SFOs get across the decision boundary. So a lot of decisions are wrong for the subcarriers on the edge, even there is no interference between orthogonal branches. By contrast, STBC-SC can still work, and outperforms the ideal STBC with no SFOs by 3~4dB. When the mean SFO estimation error is 20ppm, the degradation of STBC-SC is smaller than 1.5dB for BER = 4×10^{-4}.

From another point of view, because our SFOs self-cancellation scheme is robust to mean SFO estimation error, it is suitable to the case where the SFOs may change during the transmission of one packet.

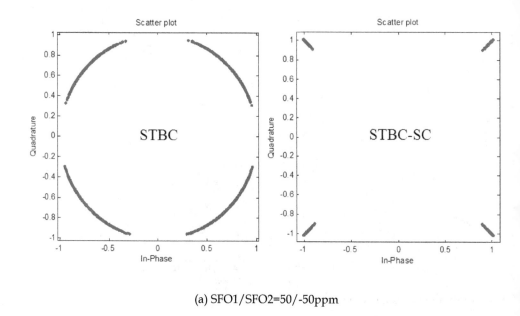

(a) SFO1/SFO2=50/-50ppm

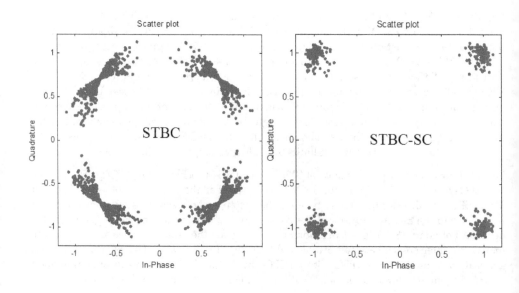

(b) SFO1/SFO2=70/-30ppm

Fig. 11. Constellations for STBC and STBC-SC with no noise

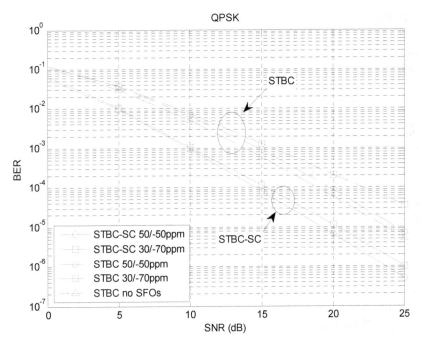

Fig. 12. BER of STBC and STBC-SC (QPSK)

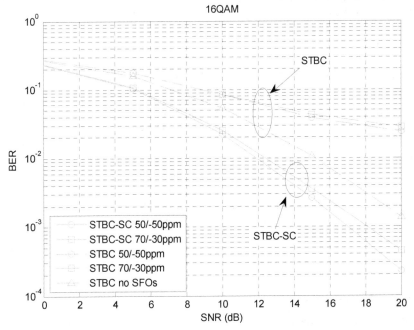

Fig. 13. BER of STBC and STBC-SC (16QAM)

5. Energy efficiency improvement and the price

Because reduced complexity directly leads to improved energy efficiency, in this section, we firstly analyze the complexity reduction brought by the self-cancellation scheme for single SFO relative to the conventional re-sampling method, and then we go to the complexity problem of the self-cancellation scheme for two SFOs in Alamouti coded OFDM based CTs. Finally, the price for the improvement is discussed in the third part.

5.1 Complexity analysis for the self-cancellation for single SFO

Taking the system in Section 4 as an example, if $N = 64$, $N_g = 16$ ($N_s = N + N_g = 80$), and one packet contains 50 OFDM symbols, the total length of one packet is 4000 samples. If the re-sampling is applied to correct a -50ppm SFO, three steps are involved (Crochiere & Rabiner, 1981): firstly, 19999 zeros are filled between each pair of input samples, which process is called interpolation; secondly, the interpolated stream goes through a low-pass filter; finally, the expected output is obtained by extracting every 20000 samples of the filtered stream, which process is called decimation. Although this complex process can be implemented efficiently by a time-varying FIR filter (Crochiere & Rabiner, 1981), because the FIR filter needs to be designed specifically for each estimated SFO, the computation complexity is still too high. For example, if the FIR filter only has 5 taps, then the generation of one sample needs 5 multiplications and 4 additions, so totally 20000 multiplications and 16000 additions are required for the whole packet.

In contrast, if the proposed self-cancellation is applied for the SFO correction, except that SFO estimation is avoided, only 32 addition operations are performed for each OFDM symbol, which means totally 32×50 = 1600 addition operations for the whole packet. We can see the synchronization complexity is reduced by over 99%, which leads to tremendous energy saving.

5.2 Complexity problem for the self-cancellation for two SFOs

As introduced in Section 1, there is no effective correction method for the two SFOs in the OFDM based CTs to our knowledge, so it's not easy to show directly the complexity reduction of the proposed scheme. However, several important facts cannot be ignored. Firstly, we just apply single re-sampling to solve the problem of two SFOs, which cannot even be solved by two re-samplings. Secondly, only single SFO estimation is performed for the purpose of re-sampling, and because our scheme is robust to the SFO estimation error, the mean SFO estimation can be an approximate version with low complexity. Thirdly, if taking the same example in Section 5.1, the complexity of the proposed scheme for two SFOs is only 1% higher than the re-sampling based correction method for single SFO in conventional OFDM systems. Based on these facts, we can say that the proposed self-cancellation scheme is still a low-cost solution for the two SFOs in Alamouti coded OFDM based CT systems.

5.3 The price for low complexity

Although the proposed schemes have low complexity, the bandwidth efficiency is cut down by half in the proposed systems due to the self-cancellation coding. In other words, we sacrifice the bandwidth efficiency for the energy efficiency. However, due to the diversity gain and array gain we get through the self-cancellation coding, the price is reduced. The simulations in (Gao & Ingram, 2010) shows that, in conventional OFDM system, the BER performance of the SFO self-cancellation scheme even outperforms the ideal OFDM system with on SFO, for the same energy per bit. But by comparing the BER performance of ideal STBC for QPSK (triangle-dashed curve in Fig. 13) and that of the STBC-SC for 16QAM (circle-solid curve in Fig. 14), we find that this advantage diminishes when the self-cancellation is applied in Alamouti coded OFDM based CTs. The reason is that the space-time coding already provides the diversity gain, so the additional improvement brought by the combining in the frequency domain cannot be as obvious as that for conventional OFDM systems.

We want to claim that, although the proposed scheme may require double time for transmitting the same amount of information because of the self-cancellation coding, it actually improve the energy efficiency of the CT system indirectly. CT itself is an energy efficient transmission technology, but the sensitivity to SFOs limits its advantages. The proposed solution to SFOs helps CT getting the best performance with additional diversity gain and array gain, which can be seen as a indirect improvement of the energy efficiency of the system. From another point of view, without a reliable solution to the SFOs problem, it's very possible that the SFOs fail the reception and a retransmission process may be activated, which will cost much more energy.

As introduced in the Section 1, because there are no other effective solutions to the problem of two SFOs in OFDM-based CT systems to our knowledge until now, we can only show the advantages of the proposed solution in terms of energy efficiency in such an indirect way. In future work, the tradeoff between the accuracy of the SFO estimation and the energy consumption should be studied carefully, so that the energy consumption of the proposed solution can be shown explicitly.

6. Summary

OFDM based Alamouti coded cooperative transmission is an efficient transmission technology in sensor networks and cellular networks, but the system is sensitive to SFOs between the transmitters and the receiver. This chapter proposed a simple method to remove the effect of the SFOs, so that the advantages of cooperative transmission can be achieved sufficiently. In this chapter, the SFO self-cancellation scheme for single SFO in conventional OFDM systems is firstly introduced. Then, after analyzing the expression of the STBC decoded symbols, we find that by adjusting the sampling frequency based on the estimated mean SFO, the self-cancellation scheme for single SFO can also work well in 2-branch STBC-OFDM systems. The drawback of this scheme is that the bandwidth efficiency is cut down by half because of the self-cancellation encoding. However, the diversity gain and array gain obtained through the self-cancellation decoding decrease this price. Simulation results show that the proposed scheme removes the phase rotation caused by the two SFOs successfully, which indirectly limits the influence of the interference between STBC branches. Our design outperforms the ideal STBC system with no SFOs, and is robust to the mean SFO estimation error, which implies that our design is suitable to the case where the SFOs may change during the transmission of one packet.

The proposed scheme brought improved energy efficiency. More specifically, when the SFO self-cancellation is applied in conventional OFDM system, the energy efficiency improvement is embedded in both the reduced synchronization complexity and the improved signal transmission efficiency; while, when the self-cancellation scheme is applied in Alamouti coded OFDM based CTs, the energy efficiency improvement is mainly shown by the low-cost synchronization process.

7. Acknowledgment

This work is supported by the National S&T Major Project (2011ZX03003-003-01). The first author also appreciates the support from the Wireless and Mobile Communication Technology R&D Center (WMRC) of Tsinghua University.

8. References

Alamouti, S.M. (1998). A simple transmit diversity technique for wireless communications, *IEEE Journal on Selected Areas in Communications*, Vol. 16, No. 8, (Oct. 1998P, pp. 1451–1458, ISSN 0733-8716.

Commission of the European Communities. (1989). Digital Land Mobile Radio Communications-COST 207. ETSI. 1989.

Crochiere, R.E. & Rabiner, L.R. (1981). Interpolation and decimation of digital signals – A tutorial review, *Proceedings of the IEEE*, Vol. 69, No. 3, (March 1981), pp. 300-331, ISSN 0018-9219.

Fechtel, S. A. (2000). OFDM carrier and sampling frequency synchronization and its performance on stationary and mobile channels, *IEEE Transactions on Consumer Electronics*, Vol. 46, No. 3, (Aug. 2000), pp. 438–441, ISSN 0098-3063.

Gao, Z. & Ingram, M. A. (2010). Self-Cancellation of Sample Frequency Offset in OFDM Systems in the Presence of Carrier Frequency Offset, *Proceedings of the 2010 IEEE 72th Vehicular Technology Conference*, pp. 1-5, ISBN 978-1-4244-3573-9, Ottawa, Canada, Sep. 6-9, 2010.

Heaton, R.; Duncan, S. & Hodson, B. (2001). A Fine Frequency and Fine Sample Clock Estimation Technique for OFDM Systems, *Proceedings of the 2001 IEEE Vehicular Technology Conference*, pp. 678-682, Rhodes, Greece, May 6-9, 2001.

Heiskala, J & Terry, J. (2002). *OFDM Wireless LANs:A Theoretical and Practical Guide.*, Sams, ISBN-10: 0672321572, Indianapolis, USA.

Horlin, F. & Bourdoux, A. (2008). *Digital Compensation for Analog Front-Ends: A New Approach to Wireless Transceiver Design*, Wiley, ISBN 978-0-470-51708-6, Chippenham, England.

IEEE (1999), Part 11: Wireless LAN Medium Access Control (MAC) and Physical Layer (PHY) Specifications, *IEEE Std 802.11a-1999*, Sep. 1999.

Kai, S.; Serpedin, E. & Ciblat, P. (2005). Decision-directed fine synchronization in OFDM systems, *IEEE Transactions on Communications*, Vol.53, No.3, (March 2005), pp.408–412, ISSN 0090-6778.

Kim, D. K.; Do, S. H.; Cho, H. B.; Chol, H. J. & Kim, K. B. (1998). A new joint algorithm of symbol timing recovery and sampling clock adjustment for OFDM systems, *IEEE Transactions on Consumer Electronics*, Vol. 44, No. 3, (Aug. 1998), pp. 1142–1149, ISSN 0098-3063.

Kleider, J.E.; Xiaoli Ma & Steenhoek, C. (2009). Distributed Multiple Antenna Carrier and Sampling Frequency Synchronization for OFDM, *Proceeding of IEEE Military Communications Conference, 2009*, pp 1-7, ISBN 978-1-4244-5238-5, Oct. 18-21 2009.

Li, Z. & Xia, X.-G. (2007). A simple Alamouti space-time transmission scheme for asynchronous cooperative systems, *IEEE Signal Processing Letters*, Vol. 14, No. 11, (Nov. 2007), pp. 804-807, ISSN 1070-9908.

Li, Z.; Xia, X.-G. & Lee, M. H. (2010). A Simple Orthogonal Space-Time Coding Scheme for Asynchronous Cooperative Systems for Frequency Selective Fading Channels, *IEEE Transactions on Communications*, Vol. 58, No. 8, (Aug. 2010), pp. 2219–2224, ISSN 0090-6778.

Liu, S.-Y. & Chong, J.-W. (2002). A study of joint tracking algorithms of carrier frequency offset and sampling clock offset for OFDM based WLANs, *Proceeding of IEEE 2002 International Conference on Communications, Circuits and Systems and West Sino Expositions*, pp. 109-113, ISBN 0-7803-7547-5.

Morelli, M. & Moretti, M. (2010). Fine Carrier and Sampling Frequency Synchronization in OFDM systems, *IEEE Transactions of Wireless Communications*, Vol. 9, No. 4, (April 2010), pp. 1514-1524, ISSN 1536-1276.

Morelli, M.; Imbarlina, G. & Moretti, M. (2010). Estimation of Residual Carrier and Sampling Frequency Offsets in OFDM-SDMA Uplink Transmissions, *IEEE Transactions on Wireless Communications*, Vol. 9, No. 2, (Feb. 2010), pp. 734-744, ISSN 1536-1276.

Nee R. & Prasad, R. (2000). *OFDM for Wireless Multimedia Communications*, Artech House, ISBN-10: 0890065306, Boston, USA.

Oberli, C. (2007). ML-based tracking algorithms for MIMO-OFDM, *IEEE Transactions on Wireless Communications*, Vol. 6, No. 7, (July 2007), pp. 2630-2639, ISSN 1536-1276.

Pollet, T. & Peeters, M. (1999). Synchronization with DMT Modulation, *IEEE Communications Magazine*, Vol. 37, No. 4, (April 1999), pp. 80-86, ISSN 0163-6804.

Pollet, T.; Spruyt, P. & Moeneclaey, M. (1994). The BER performance of OFDM systems using non-synchronized sampling, *Proceeding of 1994 IEEE Global Telecommunications Conference* , pp. 253–257, ISBN 0-7803-1820-X, Nov. 28 - Dec. 2 1994.

Sathananthan, K.; Athaudage, C.R.N. & Qiu, B. (2004). A novel ICI cancellation scheme to reduce both frequency offset and IQ imbalance effects in OFDM, *Proceeding of 2004 Ninth International Symposium on Computers and Communications*, pp: 708 – 713, ISBN 0-7803-8623-X

Shafiee, H.; Nourani, B. & Khoshgard, M. (2004). Estimation and Compensation of Frequency Offset in DAC/ADC Clocks in OFDM Systems, *Proceeding of 2004 IEEE International Conference on Communications*, pp. 2397-2401, ISBN 0-7803-8533-0, June 20-24, 2004.

Shin, O. S.; Chan, A. M.; Kung, H. T.; & Tarokh, V. (2007). Design of an OFDM cooperative space-time diversity system, *IEEE Transactions on Vehicular Technology*, Vol. 56, No. 4, July 2007, pp. 2203–2215, ISSN 0018-9545.

Simoens, S.; Buzenac, V. & De Courville, M. (2000). A new method for joint cancellation of clock and carrier frequency offsets in OFDM receivers over frequency selective channels, *Proceedings of the 2000 IEEE Vehicular Technology Conference*, pp. 390-394, ISBN 0-7803-5718-3, Tokyo, Japan, May 15-18, 2000.

Sliskovic, M. (2001). Sampling frequency offset estimation and correction in OFDM systems. *Proceeding of* 2001 *the 8th IEEE International Conference on Electronics, Circuits and Systems, 2001*, pp. 437-440, ISBN 0-7803-7057-0, Sep. 2-5, 2001.

Speth, M.; Fechtel, S.; Fock, G. & Meyr, H. (2001). Optimum receiver design for wireless broadband systems using OFDM — Part II, *IEEE Transactions on Communications*, Vol. 49, No. 4, (Apr. 2001), pp. 571-578, ISSN 0090-6778.

Speth, M.; Fechtel, S.A.; Fock, G. & Meyr, H. (1999). Optimum receiver design for wireless broadband systems using OFDM — Part I, *IEEE Transactions on Communications*, Vol. 47, No. 11, (Nov. 1999), pp. 1668-1677, ISSN 0090-6778.

Tang, S.; Gong, K. & Song, J. Pan, C. & Yang, Z. (2007). Intercarrier interference cancellation with frequency diversity for OFDM systems. *IEEE Transactions on Broadcasting*, Vol. 53, No.1, (March 2007), pp. 132-137, ISSN 0018-9316.

Zhang, W.; Li, Y.; Xia, X.-G.; Ching, P. C. & Letaief, K. B. (2008). Distributed space-frequency coding for cooperative diversity in broadband wireless ad hoc networks, *IEEE Transactions on Wireless Communications*, Vol. 7, No. 3, (Mar 2008), pp. 995-1003, ISSN 1536-1276.

Zhao, Y. & Haggman, S. G. (2001). Intercarrier interference self-cancellation scheme for OFDM mobile communication systems, *IEEE Transactions on Communications*, Vol. 49, No. 7, (Jul. 2001), pp. 1185-1191, ISSN 0090-6778.

4

The Energy Efficient Techniques in the DCF of 802.11 and DRX Mechanism of LTE-A Networks

Kuo-Chang Ting, Hwang-Cheng Wang,
Fang-Chang Kuo, Chih-Cheng Tseng and Ping Ho Ting
Minghsin University of Science and Technology
National Ilan University
National Chi Nan University
Taiwan

1. Introduction

Mobile devices such as notebooks and smart phones have replaced the personal computer as main personal information devices. These devices drive a strong demand for wireless networks and wireless communication for the rapidly growing number of Internet users. Since mobile terminals will be severely constrained by their limited battery endurance, it is essential that new protocols and control mechanisms based on the existing 802.11 standard [45] [46] [47] [48] and Long Time Evolution-Advanced (LTE-A) networks [1] [2] [3] [4] [5] [6] [7] [8] [9] [10] [11] [12] [13] [14] [15] be devised to reduce power consumption. It should be very energy efficient in 802.11 networks due to its short transmission and reception distance between stations and Access Point (AP). The characteristic of DCF is distributed, so every active station must turn on its transceiver to listen to the common share channel. It is apparent that the cost of DCF is very low due to this distributed characteristic. However, the energy efficiency of DCF is very poor due to this distributed characteristic also. Every active station must wait on this common shared channel by turning on its transceiver. It is so-called idle listening. Researchers have investigated a wide variety of techniques to limit the power consumption of the wireless network interface. Feeney and Nilsson [61] showed that an Orinoco Silver 802.11 card consumes on average, 47.4 mW with the receiver turned off (sleeping), 739.4 mW while listening to an idle channel, 900.6 mW while receiving data and 1346.2 mW while transmitting. Their results show that, unnecessary transmissions are costly, so is leaving the receiver on when it is receiving nothing. Hence, reducing the idle listening time is important for reducing the power consumption of 802.11. In the latter sections, we will illustrate that the overheads on idle listening to transmit an uplink data frame in the 802.11 networks are really extremely large especially when the number of active stations is large or the data frame is extremely short. Therefore the technique to conserve energy consumption is really very important. Fortunately the LTE and LTE-A propose the Discontinuous Reception (DRX) to conserve the energy consumption in idle listening. The DRX cycle, on-duration and sleep duration are scheduled by eNB. The UE just wakes up in the on-duration to receive possible PDCCH. If no further frame reception is indicated by PDCCH or no PDCCH is received, the user equipment (UE) can enter sleep mode in the remaining part of DRX cycle to conserve power consumption. However, the appliance of DRX might influence the QoS of some traffic such as audio and video traffics owing to the increased delay time when DRX is applied. The trade-off between the power consumption and traffics delay is a hot research issue in LTE and LTE-A networks. In later parts of this chapter, the 802.11 networks and the light sleeping mode introduced in will be introduced in section I. In order to distinguish this difference, we rename this light sleeping mode as ultra-light-sleeping mode. Then, how the ultra-light sleeping mode is applied to save the energy consumption of DCF in 802.11 networks will be introduced in section I also. A lot of energy-saving studies will be introduced in this section. In section II the LTE-A networks will be introduced roughly and the mechanism of DRX in LTE-A networks will be discussed. How the light sleeping mode or ultra-light sleeping mode is applied to the DRX of LTE-A networks will be discussed in section II also. Conclusions will be reached in section III.

2. The 802.11 networks and its energy saving techniques

2.1 The DCF of 802.11

The MAC layer of 802.11 consists of the Distributed Coordinated Function (DCF) and the Pointer Coordinated Function (PCF), which are used to coordinate stations that are simultaneously sending data. PCF, a central polling scheme in 802.11, is not mandatory in the IEEE specification; therefore it is not discussed in this article. However, the DCF of 802.11 is distributed. Once the carrier idle time exceeds the DIFS, all stations that intend to transmit frames must perform the back-off procedure to determine whether or not they can transmit their data frames. The back-off procedure is to select a random number from the interval [0, CW] where CW is the contention window, initially equal to the contention window minimum (CW$_{Min}$). Next, the stations will reduce this number by one each time an idle slot time elapses, and will freeze this counter when the channel is sensed to be busy. Once this number reaches zero, the station can then send the frame to the AP (in Infrastructure mode, also called a Point coordinator, PC), and the PC then reroutes this frame to its destination. If the PC receives this frame successfully, it will reply with an acknowledgement (ACK) frame within the Short InterFrame Space (SIFS) time. However, if the station does not receive the ACK frame from the PC within the SIFS time, collision loss may occur. The station will double its contention window and perform the back-off function again; this is what we call the exponential back-off algorithm. A diagram of the DCF is shown in Figure 1.

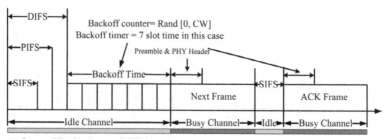

As long as idle time is over DIFS, backoff counter decreases by 1 as one idle slot time elapses. If backoff counter=0, stations can transmit the frame immediately.

Fig. 1. The mechanism of DCF

There will be at least two energy challenges in this MAC protocol. Firstly, the energy consumed for idle listening is similar to the energy consumed while receiving data [61], and a station with legacy DCF must wait through multiple DIFS idle stages if the number of active stations is large and the possibility of a successful transmission is low. This is due to the fact that too many stations may be waiting on the busy channel, but only one station can transmit its frame in the virtual Transmission Opportunity (TXOP) time. Hence, a lot of idle-listening energy will be consumed for every frame transmitted; according to calculations shown in the later sections, this energy is even larger than that consumed during collisions. Secondly, the next generation WLAN, 802.11n, will have an ultra-high PHY data rate, so the data time will be very short compared to the DIFS and back-off time. Hence, the energy efficiency and throughput will be very low ([55] [56] [58] [59] [60]), also because the data frame will be very short. In order to shorten the idle listening time, an intelligent idle listening is proposed and discussed in the latter subsection.

2.2 Intelligent idle listening mode

To raise the energy efficiency of 802.11, Ting et al. [79] proposed an intelligent idle-listening and ultra-light sleeping mode to reduce the energy consumption during the DIFS and back-off idle time. The propose lets the mobile devices wake up for a short period of time, e.g. $1\mu s$, at the beginning and the end of a DIFS interval. Two intelligent schemes for idle-channel (space) checking are proposed. The scale of modern integrated circuit design can be as low as 65 nm so far, so $1\mu s$ should be long enough for devices to decide whether or not the channel is busy. In fact, the transceiver system consists of the antenna, clock recovery, amplifier, FFT, demodulation, interleaving (if necessary) and decoding. However, the energy consumed in the antenna and amplifier constitutes a large part of the total energy consumed, e.g. 95%. We can design a power switch on the antenna and amplifier to determine whether the system is in a light sleeping mode or a normal idle-listening mode. If the switch is on, the DCF is in the idle-listening mode. Conversely, the DCF is in the light sleeping mode if the switch is off. If the DCF is in the ultra-light sleeping mode, the time to wake up should be very short due to a very short switch time. The schematic diagram for this switch is shown in Figure 2.

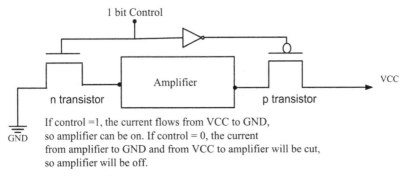

Fig. 2. Schematic diagram of the amplifier switch

The DIFS of DCF shown in Figure 1 is 34 μs for 802.11a and 802.11n. In fact, the only work done during the idle-listening period is space checking, i.e. judging whether the channel being listened to is idle or not. In order to reduce the power consumption, we can use the fact that we do not need to receive the data from the antenna, clock recovery, amplifier, demodulation, FFT and the decoder. Instead, we only need to check the space time in the PHY layer. On the other hand, if the first microsecond is found to be 'space', and the last microsecond of *DIFS* is also found to be 'space', then the station can be sure that the *DIFS* idle time has been long enough. In this situation, the DCF of the station can begin performing the normal back-off operation. The implementation is addressed in the following steps.

Step 1. The beginning of space checking:

The normal procedures of DCF in space checking are antenna receiving, clock recovery, amplifying, demodulation, FFT, and decoding. If the decoding results for the time interval is 'space' (no data in), then the DCF of this station can be sure that this is a 'space' time interval. We propose two fast schemes for deciding whether or not it is a 'space' time interval. Firstly, we can use *SNR* threshold sensed by a low power sensor. Below this threshold, we can be certain that this is a 'space' time interval. Secondly, if the data sub-carriers of the OFDM symbol are 'space' (if an OFDM scheme is applied), we can be sure that it is a 'space' time interval. However, if **only one sub-carrier is non-space for the OFDM symbol**, it may be assumed to be **interference noise** (RFID or microwave radiation) in some frequency band. Hence, we can verify this 'space' time interval within 1 μs.

Step 2. Entering the light sleeping mode:

Once the station knows that it is a 'space' time interval, the station can enter light sleeping mode by turning off this one bit switch as shown in Figure 2. If we assume the pre-wakeup time and wake-up time (Amplifier's stable time) to be w and ϕ μs respectively, we can set the wake-up timer to ($DIFS - w - \varphi - 2$).

Step 3. The end of space checking:

When the station is awakened by the timer, it will check whether or not the channel is 'space'. If the channel is idle, the station can perform the back-off operation according to the DCF standard. *However, if the channel is not idle, the AP might have sent a series of training symbols to synchronize the destined station after the* Point Interframe Space *(PIFS) time shown in Figure 1 since the beginning of DIFS. This* preamble time for 802.11a or non-HT 802.11n is around 16 μs, which should be long enough for the stations to respond to the AP's synchronization message. It is the reason why that the station can enter the light sleeping mode without needing to notify the AP that it will enter the Power-Saving Mode (PSM) according to the 802.11 standard. The timing diagram is shown in Figure 3.

The energy consumed during back-off idle listening also plays an important role in determining the power consumption of 802.11. In fact, this intelligent idle-listening scheme can be applied to the back-off. The station can check the space in the beginning of one slot time, and sleep and then be awakened by the sleep timer as the end of this slot time. To lengthen the sleep time, we adopt two-slot time strategy. In other words, the station can check the space in the beginning of the first slot time, and wake up in the end of the second slot time. If the station detects the channel being idle, it could decrease its back-off counter

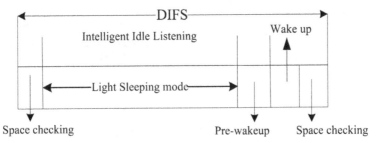

Fig. 3. Intelligent idle-listening in the DIFS period

by two, else it decreases its counter by one. If the beginning of the first slot time is not idle, the station must freeze this counter. It is apparent that if the counter is only one, the station must use the one-slot time strategy. We show this scheme as in Figure 4.

In fact, the idle listening can be divided into several categories. If the station is waiting for the *DIFS* idle time after a successful transmission between another station and the AP, this idle-listening time is different to the *SIFS* idle time, which is the turnaround time between a transmitter and a receiver. As the PHY data rate becomes higher, the data time will become shorter. For example, if the frame size is up to 600 octets, and the PHY data rate is up to 600 *Mbps*, the real data time not including preamble and the PHY header will be as short as 8 μs. This data time is even shorter than one slot time under 802.11n. Therefore, it is suggested that the receiver may not apply this efficient power scheme during this critical *SIFS* time.

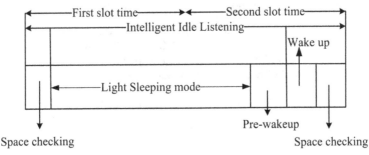

Fig. 4. The two-slot time strategy for space checking in the back-off.

2.3 Reference design of the amplifier

2.3.1 The amplifier stable time

A power amplifier is a circuit for converting an input signal and DC power into an output signal of significantly higher output power for transmission and receiving in a radio system; it is an important circuit component used in 802.11 PHY design. In fact, the amplifier under the 802.11 standard is composed of many capacitors, resistors, and other circuits. The charging time of the capacitors is critical to the stable time of the amplifier. From [82], we can see that the amplifier stable time does not exceed 2 μs. Figure 5 illustrates the power amplifier design in [82]. In order to resolve the compatibility issue, we set this amplifier stable time, i.e. wake-up time w to be 2 μs.

Reference Design:

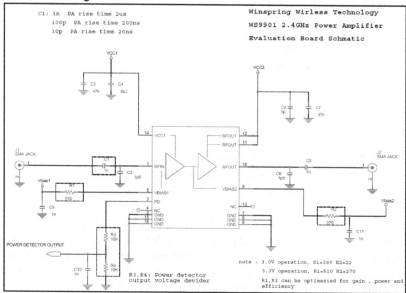

Fig. 5. The reference design of the power amplifier.

2.3.2 The switch time of the amplifier

The switch time of the amplifier is critical to the success of this scheme, so it is essential for us to evaluate it through the analysis and SPICE simulation. If we assume that the total power of the amplifier, P, is 1300 mW, and the total capacitance, C, is about 95 nF, as shown in Figure 5, we can obtain the switch time using Equation (1).

$$\Delta T = C \times \Delta V / I = C \times \Delta V / (P / Vdd) \tag{1}$$

We can obtain Equation (2) from Equation (1).

$$T = C \times Vdd^2 / P \tag{2}$$

If Vdd is 3 V and 3.3 V as shown in Figure 5, the switch time is 657 and 796 ns respectively according to Equation (2). The results obtained from Equations (1) and (2) match with the results of our SPICE simulation. Hence, if we assume the pre-wakeup time of the amplifier to be 1 μs, this should be long enough to switch this amplifier.

2.4 Energy efficiency of DCF

If we let $idle_p$, $recv_p$, $trans_p$, $light_p$, $sleep_e$, P, R, R_{basic}, φ, ϕ, and s denote powers for idle listening, receiving, transmission, light sleeping mode, sleeping mode, packet length (in bits), data rate, basic data rate, all PHY overheads in data, an ACK transmission time, and an OFDM symbol time respectively, we can calculate the energy efficiencies in the MAC layer as shown in the following subsections.

2.4.1 Energy efficiency limit of typical DCF

If the number of active stations is very small, the energy consumed in idle listening during the DIFS period and the back-off stage is not large. If there is only one active station, it needs only one DIFS period of idle listening for every frame transmission. If the station is very lucky and sets the back-off counter to zero, we can get the energy efficiency limit of DCF, DCF_{eff}, as shown in Equation (3)

$$DCF_{eff} = \frac{\lceil (P/R)/s \rceil \times s \times trans_p}{[\varphi + \lceil (P/R)/s \rceil \times s) \times trans_p + idle_p \times (DIFS + SIFS) + (\phi + \lceil (ACK/R_{basic})/s \times s \rceil) \times recev_p} \quad (3)$$

where $\lceil x \rceil$ denotes the smallest integer larger than x. For example, if the frame size is up to 2304 octets, and the data rate is 54 $Mbps$ for non-HT 802.11n, the DCF_{eff} will be 81%. However, if the data rate is up to 600 $Mbps$ (for MCS 31 PHY mode, 40 MHz bandwidth, number of spatial streams=4, 64 QAM modulation), and the basic data rate is only 60 $Mbps$ (for MCS 24 PHY mode with BPSK modulation), the DCF_{eff} will be only 19.67% because of the short data time if we assume the idle-listening power, transmission power, receiving power, and sleeping power to be 0.89W, 1.4W, 1.02W, and 0.05W respectively, based on [61]. If the number of spatial streams is greater than one, we assume that all energy consumed in idle listening, receiving, and transmission will be multiplied by this number of spatial streams, based on MIMO technology.

2.4.2 Average energy efficiency of typical DCF

It is apparent that if the number of active stations is large, the waiting idle time will increase tremendously, since there will be multiple stages of the DIFS idle time and large contention window sizes. The idle time in the $DIFS_t^M$ DIFS, , can be expressed through Equation (4) where M and P_s denote the number of active stations and the possibility of successful transmission respectively, based on Bianchi's model [35]. Let be the total $DIFS_t^M$ DIFS idle time needed for a station to transmit a frame when M active stations are contesting for the channel. It can be calculated using Equation (4).

$$DIFS_t^M = ((1 - P_s)/P_s + 1) \times DIFS \times M \quad (4)$$

We can reduce Equation (4) to Equation (5):

$$DIFS_t^M = (M/P_s) \times DIFS \quad (5)$$

It must be emphasized that P_s is a function of M. If $M=1$, $P_s =1$ (perfect channel is assumed), and $DIFS_t^M =DIFS$. However, if M is large, P_s will be very low and $DIFS_t^M$ will increase tremendously. Now, we can find the energy consumed during idle listening of DIFS, $DIFS_e^M$ from Equation (6).

$$DIFS_e^M = DIFS_t^M \times Idle_p \quad (6)$$

To analyze other power consumption factors such as back-off and collision costs, we express these two consumption factors in Equations (7) and (8), where τ, p, R, S_t, φ and m denote the probability that a station transmits in a randomly chosen slot time, conditional collision probability, data rate, one OFDM symbol time, all PHY overheads and total back-off stages, respectively. Hence, the total energy consumption for one frame transmission, $Total\_e$, including the energy consumed during the DIFS, back-off, collision, receiving, transmission, and SIFS idle listening can be calculated accurately using Equation (9), where $Tran_t$ and Ack_t denote the transmission time of one data frame and an ACK frame respectively, both including the PHY overheads.

$$Backoff_t^M = W_{\min}(\sum_{i=0}^{m-1}((2p)^i) + \frac{(2p)^m}{1-p})$$ (7)

$$Coll_t^M = (\varphi + \lceil (8P / R) / S_t \rceil \times S_t) \times ((1 - P_s) / P_s) \times (2 + 3C_3^M \tau^3 (1 - \tau)^{M-3})$$ (8)

$$Total\_e = Tran_p(Coll_t^M + Tran_t) + Recv_p(Ack_t) + Idle_p(DIFS_t^M + Backoff_t^M + SIFS)$$ (9)

2.4.3 The intelligent idle-listening scheme

If we let s_t, φ, and w_l denote the space checking time, pre-wakeup time and wake-up time respectively, the reduced ratio, κ_{DIFS}, can be expressed through Equation (10), if we assume that $(2 s_t + w_l + \varphi) < DIFS$.

$$\kappa_{DIFS} = \frac{(2s_t + \varphi + w_l) \times Idle_p + (DIFS - \varphi - w_l - 2s_t) \times light_p}{DIFS \times Idle_p}$$ (10)

Hence, the idle energy, $In\_DIFS_e^M$, consumed in this DIFS by applying this intelligent scheme, can be expressed through Equation (11).

$$In\_DIFS_e^M = \kappa_{DIFS} \times DIFS_e^M$$ (11)

If $light_p$ is close to $idle_p$, κ_{DIFS} is not significantly small, as can be seen from Equation (10). Furthermore, if $(2s_t + \varphi + w_l) > DIFS$, then it is not possible to implement our scheme. Fortunately, we present two intelligent schemes for space checking in this article, and we also propose a quick switch system for wakeup. The time for space checking and the pre-wakeup time of the amplifier are up to 1 μs and 2 μs respectively, as shown in the previous section. Hence, this limitation should not pose a problem. Furthermore, the power consumed in the antenna and the amplifier constitutes a large part of the total energy consumed in the transceiver. Hence, $light_p$ should be much smaller than $idle_p$, and not much larger than $sleep_p$. The κ_{DIFS} in Equation (10) is about 20% based on our analyses and simulations. If we apply this intelligent idle listening scheme to the back-off, the reduced ratio, $\kappa_{Back-off}$ by means of the two-slot time strategy, can be expressed through Equation (12).

$$\kappa_{Back-off} = \frac{2s_t \times Idle_p + (2slot - \varphi - w_l - 2s_t) \times light_p}{2slot \times Idle_p}$$ (12)

$\kappa_{Back-off}$ is about 32.37%. Here, the total time of the two slots is 18 μs for the 802.11a and 802.11n.

2.5 Simulation and results

2.5.1 Simulation environment

The IEEE 802.11n standard [48] employs multi-input multi-output orthogonal frequency division multiplexing (MIMO-OFDM) transmission techniques to enable high throughput communications, so that a 600 *Mbps PHY data rate* can be attained through a channel with a bandwidth of 40 MHz [48]. Other features of this new 802.11n standard applicable at both transmitting and receiving ends are a 400 *ns* short guard interval, transmit beam-forming, HT greenfield format, a maximum HT PSDU length of up to 65535 octets through the aggregation — MSDU (A-MSDU) (or aggregation-MPDU (A-MPDU)) technique, HT-PMD sublayer and space-time block codes (STBC). The PPDU format transmitted by a High Throughput (HT) STA is determined by the TXVECTOR FORMAT, CH_BANDWIDTH, CH_OFFSET and MCS parameters listed in the PHY-TXSTART.request service primitive. There are totally three frame formats; the *Non-HT format*, the *HT mixed format*, and the *HT greenfield format* as shown in Figure 6 [48]. The simulated parameters of 802.11n are listed in Table 1. In this chapter, we select the common HT mixed PPDU format as the simulation target, since it is compatible with non-HT standards, 802.11a/b/g. This mixed format carries a heavier PHY overhead than the non-HT standards. All uplink traffic except ftp, transmission of e-mail attachments, HDTV and video conferencing transmissions have a small frame size, e.g. TCP connections, DNS lookups, MAC layer control frames, and web page requests. We assume that we use the A-MPDU technique to aggregate all these small frames into one large frame with a size of up to 2700 octets.

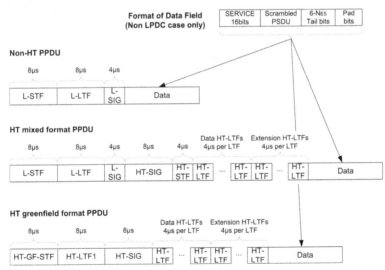

Fig. 6. The PPDU formats proposed in 802.11n [48].

2.5.2 Power analysis and simulation under DCF

The analysis and simulation results of MAC efficiency and the probability of successful transmission are illustrated in Figure 7, based on the relevant parameters given in Table 1. Figure 7 shows that the results of the analysis are very close to that of the simulations.

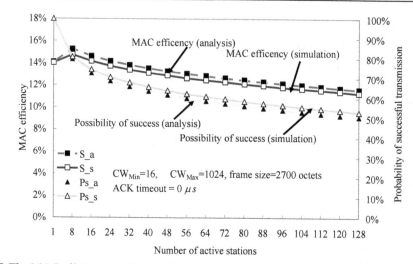

Fig. 7. The MAC efficiency and probability of transmission of the DCF of 802.11n.

SlotTime (t_{slot})	9 μs	Number of spatial streams (N_{SS})	4 (EQM)
SIFS	16 μs	MCS index	31
AirPropagationTime (δ)	1 μs	Modulation	64-QAM
aPreambleLength	16 μs	Coding rate	5/6
Legacy Short Ttraining Field (L-STF)	8 μs	N_{BPSC} (i_{SS}) (Number of coded bits per single carrier for each spatial stream, i_{SS} = 1, ..., N_{SS})	6
Legacy Long Ttraining Field (L-LTF)	4 μs	N_{SD} (Number of data subcarriers)	108
High Throughput SIGNAL field	8 μs	N_{SP} (Number of pilot subcarriers)	6
aLTFTwoLength	4 μs	N_{CBPS} Number of coded bits per OFDM symbol	2592
Legacy SIGNAL field (H_1)	4 μs	N_{DBPS} Number of data bits per OFDM symbol	2160
aPLCPSigTwoLength	8 μs	N_{ES} (Number of BCC encoders for the DATA field)	2
PSDU MaxLength	65535 octets	GI (Guard interval)	400 ns
PPDU MaxTime	10 ms	PHY Data rate	600 Mbps
aCWmin	15	PHY Basic Data rate	60 Mbps
aCWmax	1023	Bandwidth	40 MHz
Frame size	2700 octets	Number of active stations	1, 2, 4, 8, 16, 32, 64, 128

Table 1. The relevant parameters of 802.11n

Hence, this shows that our simulations are accurate. From Figure 7, it can also be seen that the probability of successful transmission will decrease as the number of active stations increases. Hence, the MAC capacity will decrease from 15.6% to 11.3% as the number of active stations increase from 1 to 128. The maximum MAC efficiency is observed when the number of active stations is 4, not 1. However, the number of DIFS stages needed for a station to send a frame will increase as the probability of successful transmission decreases. In order to evaluate the total energy consumption, we simulate and analyze three kinds of energy consumption factors including the DIFS, back-off idle listening, and collisions in Figure 8. Here, D_e_a and D_e_s stand for the energy consumed in DIFS idle listening as obtained through analyses and simulations respectively. So are the labels such as BA_e_a, BA_e_s (BA stands for back-off), C_e_a, and C_e_s (C stands for collision). We assume that the stations send and receive frames using the fixed-power scheme, so these energy consumption factors such as the energy consumed in transmission, receiving, and SIFS idle listening are fixed if the PHY data rate and frame size are fixed. Hence, we can obtain a precise energy consumption model for one successful frame transmission.

Figure 8 also shows that the results of simulation are very similar to those obtained through analyses. It can also be seen that the time and energy consumed in the DIFS, instead of collision, will grow exponentially as the number of active stations increases. The energy consumed during back-off idle listening will also increase tremendously when the number of active stations increases. We attribute this to the fact that for a station, due to a large number of collisions, there will be a high probability that it will get a large contention window based on the exponential back-off algorithm defined in 802.11. If we apply the reference design in Figure 5 and the intelligent idle listening to the listening of the wireless stations during the DIFS and back-off period, the time taken for space checking, pre-wakeup, and, wakeup in Figure 3 are set to 1 μs, 2 μs, and 1 μs respectively, then we can obtain the total energy, total DIFS energy, R_tot_e_s (total energy after reduction), R_D_e_s (DIFS energy after reduction), R_BA_e_s (back off energy after reduction), and reduced ratio of total energy as in Figure 9, and Figure 10 respectively.

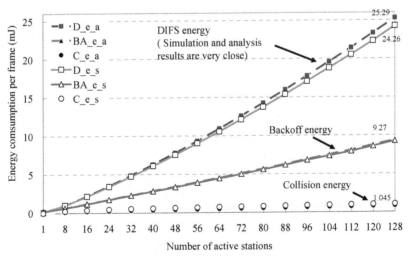

Fig. 8. The key energy consumption factors in the DCF of 802.11n

Figure 9 shows that a station not applying the intelligent idle listening scheme will consume 35.3 *mJ* for one frame transmission if the number of active stations is 128; whereas, a station using the intelligent idle-listening scheme will consume only 9.7 *mJ*. This is due to the fact that the energy consumption during DIFS idle listening will be reduced from 24.3 *mJ* to 4.9 *mJ* and the energy consumption during back-off listening will be reduced from 9.2 *mJ* to 3.0 *mJ* for one frame transmission. Figure 10 shows that if the number of active stations is one, the reduction is close to 21.3%. However, as the number of active stations increases, the probability of successful transmission will decrease. Hence, the collision penalty will increase tremendously, and the energy consumed in DIFS idle listening during the collision

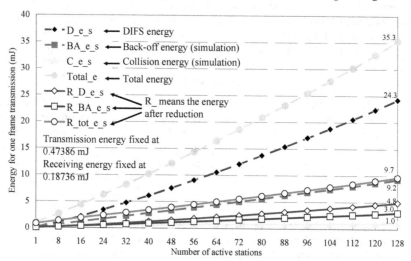

Fig. 9. The total energy and the total energy after reduction due to the application of the intelligent idle-listening scheme for one frame transmission.

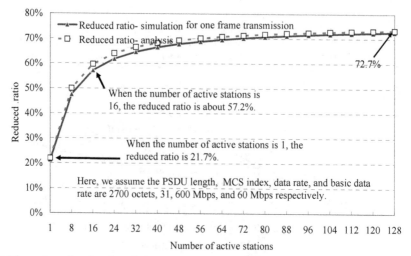

Fig. 10. The reduced ratio of total energy

stage will increase for M active stations. The total energy consumed in the DIFS idle listening is proportional to M and is inversely proportional to the probability of successful transmission according to Equations (4) and (5). The energy consumed in the back-off idle listening will also increase tremendously due to high average contention window according to the exponential back-off function defined in 802.11. So, when the number of active stations increases, the energy consumed in the DIFS and back-off will dominate other power consumption factors and the reduction in total energy will be higher if applying this intelligent scheme. Figure 10 also shows that if the number of active stations is 1, 16, and 128, the total energy consumption for one frame transmission decreases by 21.3%, 57.2%, and 72.7% respectively.

2.6 Related works

2.6.1 The power-saving techniques for stations with no active data transmission

The 802.11 standard employs a different approach to energy conservation with its Power-Saving Mode (PSM) ([45] [46] [47] [48]). The 802.11 provides a mechanism for a power-constrained client to save power by notifying the station to enter the PSM. During the PSM, the station can turn the radio on and off in regular intervals to receive the traffic indication map (TIM) in the beacon broadcast by AP. If the TIM indicates that the AP is buffering frames for the station, the station must retrieve its frame by sending a power-save poll (PS_Poll) to the AP. In fact, if a station first connects with the AP by sending an association request, AP will send an association response with an association ID (AID) to this station. Hence, if there is any data frame destination for this station buffered in AP, the xth bit of TIM will be 1, else it will be 0 where x is equal to the AID of this station. The timing for the stations to wake up and receive the beacon frame is based on the beacon interval field in the received beacon frame. Readers can find that stations can enter sleeping mode and wake up based on this beacon interval. Therefore it can save a lot of energy consumed. Krashinsky et al. [54] evaluates the PSM and found that stations can save the energy consumption up to 90% but stations must pay the delay cost to download the web page. If an idle station with no active data to be uploaded neither to be downloaded, the station will waste the energy consumption on receiving the beacon frame and in switching from sleep to wakeup. In order to solve this tradeoff between energy consumption and traffic delay, they proposed the Bounded Slowdown (BSD) Protocol. Stations can decrease the frequency of wakeup from sleeping mode to receive beacon frames when they are aware of user being occupied in think time in browsing a web page based on this protocol. Stations can save power consumptions with the bounded delay for data frame transmission based on BSD, but its power consumption is still higher than that of PSM. Furthermore, this protocol focuses on the case of long user's think time when users browse web pages, but this case is rare in real situation. Therefore, they proposed Cross-Layer Power Manager (XEM) to distinguish user think time from inter-arrival time of data frames, in other words, BSD and PSM are used iteratively to save power consumptions. But this burdens the duty of application to achieve this cross-layer communication.

Qiao and Shin [30] proposed Smart Power-Saving Mode (SPMS), an enhanced version of BSD. The key idea of SPMS is that stations listen to the beacon frames broadcast by AP on BSD protocol by static method during the period of idle time, but the evaluation of idle time is dynamic. However, the power consumption of SPSM is still higher than that of PSM, but the reduced delay time is very limited. Compared with BSD and SPMS, Dynamic Beacon Period algorithm (DBP) [71] can be used in any possible idle time because DBP saves power consumption by turning off the wireless interface. Stations having no data frames to be sent are idle stations, so they can enter sleeping mode. Owing to the calling procedure from distant stations by Peer to Peer (P2P) or voice applications such as Skype, stations must connect to the Internet by listening to the beacon frames broadcast by AP. Ye, Heidemann, and Estrin introduced S-Mac [84] suggested a media access control algorithm for low power sensors which trades latency and throughput for a reduction in power consumption. S-Mac may significantly increase the battery-power sensor lifetime, but in doing so, it incurs a throughput penalty proportional to the power saving. Jim Snow et al. [53] proposed a low power TDMA protocol over 802.11. The key idea behind their scheme is that the controller allocates timeslots to its clients, during which the clients may send and receive from the controller. This scheme is an ideal power-saving scheme, but it involves high complexity and cost due to its centralized-control approach. Takiguchi [78] describes the design and implementation of a wireless wake-up module that uses this ID matching mechanism. Simulation results reveal that the wake-up module consumes only 12.4 μW while idle listening, and that employing this Bloom-filter-based approach eliminates 99.95 % of power consumption in their application scenarios. This Bloom filter is by embedding a single-chip, CC1000 [80]. into the wakeup module of wireless communication. The power consumption of this module is much less than that consumed in idle listening. The architecture proposed by Takiguchi can be illustrated by Figures 11 and 12.

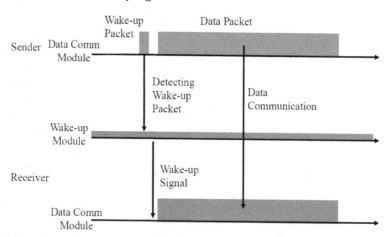

Fig. 11. Wake-up communication scheme

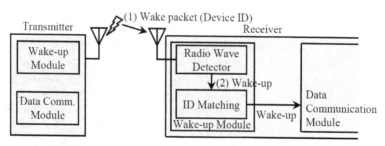

Fig. 12. A two-stage wake-up communication scheme

This scheme indeed can reduce the power consumption in idle listening, but it needs additional wake-up module for the reception and transmission. Moreover, it needs to send additional packets for wakeup, so it cannot be compatible with the legacy 802.11 stations without wakeup module or the stations not in sleeping mode.

2.6.2 power-saving techniques for stations with active data transmission

The stations without any uploaded packets can use the techniques listed above to save power consumption, but it is useless for the stations with ready packets to be sent. In fact, as stated above, during the back-off stage, only one station will succeed in accessing the channel. The others will wait until the ongoing frame transmission is finished. In 802.11, this waiting time is conveyed by Network Allocation Vector (NAV) and can be obtained from the RTS/CTS frame [45]. Different from the original definition of NAV, the DIFS after a successful frame transmission is added to the NAV to further conserve the energy. Thus, if an RTS frame is heard by certain active stations, these active stations will set their NAVs upon the reception of the MAC header of the RTS frame. They then set their wakeup timers to the NAV minus the time to wake up and enter light sleeping mode. However, if an active station is a hidden terminal, it is deaf to the RTS frame but will hear the CTS frame that responds to the RTS frame. The hidden active station can then set its NAV upon receiving the MAC header of the CTS frame where the NAV includes the DIFS idle time if our intelligent scheme is applied. The scheme is shown in Figure 13.

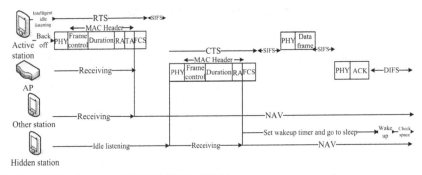

Fig. 13. The NAV scheme with RTS/CTS in 802.11

This technique has been described in the standard of 802.11. Wang et al. [81] and Sun et al. [83] have illustrated this concept in detail and name this scheme as Demand Wakeup MAC (DW-MAC).

As defined in 802.11 [45], when a station receives a frame that is not destined for it, it will set the NAV according to the duration/ID field (in microseconds) of the received frame plus SIFS, the time to transmit an ACK frame including the PHY overhead, and DIFS minus the wakeup and pre-wakeup time to perform space checking. After that, it sets the wake up timer and then enters light sleeping mode. This NAV scheme is depicted in Figure 14. As shown in Figure 14, other busy listening stations must wake up before the end of the DIFS minus the wake up and pre-wakeup time to perform space checking. If the duration is not specified by the sender, for instance, in power save poll messages, the duration can be estimated as follows:

$$Duration = \lceil (W / R) / S_t \rceil \times S_t - S_t \qquad (13)$$

where W, R, and S_t denote the length of PLCP Protocol Data Unit (PPDU), the data rate for PHY header, and one OFDM symbol time respectively, and $\lceil \bullet \rceil$ denotes the ceiling function. Note that, as shown in Figure 5, the HT-PHY overheads such as high throughput long training field (HT-LTF) depend on the frame format and are included in the PHY sublayer service data units (PSDU) of 802.11n. As a result, the duration given in (13) must be decreased by these HT-PHY overheads.

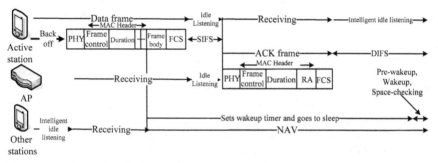

Fig. 14. A NAV scheme for the frame without RTS/CTS.

3. The LTE-A networks and its energy saving techniques

3.1 Introduction to LTE-A networks and DRX

The evolving fourth-generation (4G) wireless technologies, such as long term evolution (LTE) of Universal Mobile Telecommunications System (UMTS) and WiMAX offer high bandwidth for data transfer. These high data rates over the access part of the network are achieved through the use of higher order modulation, such as 64-quadrature amplitude modulation (QAM), advanced coding techniques, convolutional turbo codes combined with advanced antenna techniques, such as multiple-input multiple-output (MIMO), space-division multiple access (SDMA), and so on. The receivers require computationally complex circuitry that drains the user equipment (UE)'s battery power quickly, thus limiting the use of enriched 4G services. There are various methods, such as DRX in LTE and idle/sleep modes in WiMAX, introduced to improve UE battery lifetime. Furthermore, DRX offers significant improvement with respect to resource utilization, particularly for applications characterized by extended OFF periods. Based on the application type, the DRX parameters are selected so that the energy and resource savings can be maximized. However, the cost associated with enabling DRX modes is that there will be extended delay when the UE needs to transmit/receive data. There may be some Peer-To-Peer (P2P) requests from the distant peer stations and these requests will be delayed from these power saving modes. Therefore there is a need to select the DRX parameters prudently to balance the cost associated with the ensuing limited packet delay and the maximal power saving.

In DRX mode, the UE powers down most of its circuitry when there are no packets to be transmitted or received. During this time UE listens to the downlink (DL) occasionally and may not keep in sync with uplink (UL) transmission depending on whether the UE is registered with an evolved node-B (eNB) in radio resource control (RRC) connected or not RRC idle state [9]. Furthermore, UE has to perform scanning of the neighboring eNB in the event of detecting signal quality degradation with respect to the serving eNB. If the signal quality from one of neighboring eNBs is better than the serving eNB, UE should come out of DRX mode to perform handover (HO) if the UE is in RRC_CONNECTED state or perform a cell reselection if the UE is in RRC_IDLE state. UE may choose to go into DRX once the handover/cell reselection is successfully performed. While in the RRC_IDLE state, UE has to perform tracking area (TA) update whenever a change in TA is detected. In fact, DRX is not a novel idea in Long Term Evolution (LTE) [9] since it has been applied in the 2nd generation system, e.g. the Global System for Mobile Communications (GSM). LTE and LTE-A) are currently two main research focuses, both of which adopt DRX in their specifications. Bontu and Illidge [25] model the LTE DRX and prove that the LTE DRX achieves a more power saving gain over Universal Mobile Telecommunications System (UMTS) DRX at the cost of prolonged delay to wake up. However, as shown in the previous paragraph, some types of traffics such as voices and video are very delay-sensitive and meeting the demand of requirements of Quality of Service (QoS) is essential to these traffics. Owing to the fact that the inter-packet arrival time of these traffics are short, it is impossible for UEs to go to sleep and wake up from this deep sleeping mode. In fact, this transition requires energy and it also takes time, so it needs criteria for these UEs to decide whether go to sleep or not after the expiration of inactive timer (I-Timer) in the DRX cycle. In this chapter, the concept of light sleeping mode [79] is also applied to shorten this wakeup time and reduce transition energy.

Here, the light sleeping mode is defined as that all components in the transceivers of UE are not turned off except the amplifier. This sleeping mode is especially useful when the UE enter into a very short DRX cycle. This light sleeping is distinguished from the definition in other common researches [65]. In fact, some researchers also have the light sleeping mode in their article, but the definition is unclear. Some researchers might regard their light sleeping mode as that stations (used in 802.11) or user equipment (UE, used in LTE) reduce its power consumption by reducing the power level of amplifier in RF for idle listening. They might regard the light sleeping mode as cutting down the circuitry of the transceiver of UE, but the deep sleeping mode is defined in their articles as turning off all the circuitries of UE in transceivers only. In fact, considering the RF power only is impractical in real cases. In this chapter, the powers of circuitries which are cut off include all RF parts except the timer circuitry in deep sleeping mode. The wakeup time from deep sleeping mode also includes the stable time of all wakeup circuitries, the ready time of driver to run in CPU of UEs, and the reception time of important system information of eNB. As to the question that how long of the DRX cycle to sustain the deep sleeping, light sleeping or not entering into sleeping mode in this DRX cycle is the one of key motivations discussed in this chapter.

3.2 The mechanism of DRX in LTE-A networks

3.2.1 DRX

The DRX mechanism in LTE adopts UE-specific parameters determined by the evolved Node B (eNB) (Namely each UE has its own DRX configuration). These parameters are described as follows without taking into account the influence brought by retransmissions and possible measurement gaps.

- I-Timer: Specifies the number of consecutive physical downlink control channel (PDCCH) subframe(s) during which the receiver will be opened after successfully decoding a PDCCH, indicating an initial uplink (UL) or DL transmission.
- On-Duration Timer (O-Timer): Specifies the number of consecutive PDCCH subframe(s) at the beginning of a DRX cycle.
- DRX cycle: Specifies periodic repetitions of the on-duration. A UE can be configured by two DRX cycles at most (short DRX cycle and long DRX cycle).

The UE monitors PDCCH during the on-duration period, during which the O-Timer is running. If there is no DL transmission for this UE, it will turn off its receiver and enter the sleeping mode instantly after the O-Timer expires. If the PDCCH indicates an initial UL or DL data transmission (here this kind of PDCCH means a valid PDCCH), the ITimer will be started to keep the UE awake to continue monitoring the PDCCH for possible DL traffic. While another valid PDCCH is received during the inactivity period when the I-Timer is running, the I-Timer will be restarted to prolong the inactivity period. However, if the UE has no data transfer in a certain period (i.e. the duration of I-Timer), it will switch off the receiver and won't switch it on until the next on-duration period. During the sleep period, all DL data for this UE will be buffered in the eNB and this UE won't be scheduled before the forthcoming on-duration period. The active time of this process stands for the time when the UE keeps monitoring the PDCCH, which includes the time when either the O- or I-Timer is running (on-duration period and inactivity period).

An example mechanism of DRX is shown in Figure 15 [25].

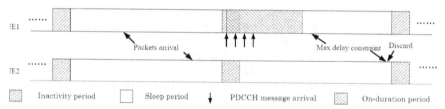

Fig. 15. An example mechanism of DRX.

The critical problem of this DRX mechanism is that if the duration from the expiration of the I-Timer to the next DRX cycle is very short, it is not suitable for the UEs to enter deep sleep in this period due to the energy overheads of this transition and time limitation in DRX cycle. This improper scheduling is illustrated shown in Figure 16.

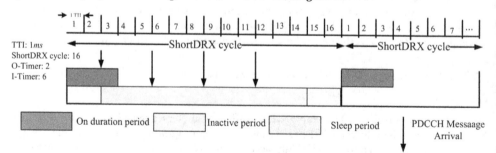

Fig. 16. An example of improper scheduling in DRX.

Figure 16 shows that if the O-timer, I-Timer, and DRX cycle are 2, 6, 16 respectively, the UE is suggested not to enter sleep at the moment of I-Timer expiration if the traffic run in this UE is with delay-sensitive characteristic. If the wakeup time is longer than that of this sleep period, UE may not enter sleep or just go to light-sleeping mode only. In this example, the scheduled sleeping-period is short to $2ms$. However, the wakeup time for the UE from deep sleeping mode to active mode may be up to $100ms$ [62] and the transition energy needed to wakeup may be up to $100mJ$ if we assume the average power of this transition is up $1W$. This energy consumption is much higher than that consumed in idle state for the UE. Furthermore, the traffics such as VoIP might suffer from too numerous delay jitters due to this sleeping action.

3.2.2 PDCCH

The UE will obtain from the PDCCH information for both uplink and downlink resource allocations the UE may use. The Down Link Control Information (DCI) mapped on the PDCCH has different formats and depending on the size DCI is transmitted using one or more Control Channel Elements (CCEs). A CCE is equal to 9 resource element groups. Each group in turn consists of 4 resource elements. The different PDCCH formats are shown in Table 2, where it can be seen that as PDCCH is using QPSK modulation, then a single resource element carries 2 bits and there are 8 bits in a resource element group. The UE will listen to the set of PDCCHs and tries to decode them (checking all formats) in all subframes. The set of PDCCHs to monitor is up to 6 channels. Depending on the network parameterization, some of the PDCCHs are so-called common PDCCHs and may also contain power control information. A subframe in LTE-A consists of ten subframes and each subframe consists of 2 slots. In general, one slot consists of 6-7 OFDM symbols depending on the duration of cyclic prefixes (CP), used to avoid the inter-symbol interference (ISI). If a short CP, 5.2 µs, is used, one slot time consists of 7 OFDM time, but one slot consists of 6 OFDMs if an extended CP, 16.7 µs, is used. The structure of a frame in LTE-A network is illustrated in Figure 17.

PDCCH format	Number of CCEs	Number of resource element groups	Number of PDCCH bits
0	1	9	72
1	2	18	144
2	4	36	288
3	8	72	576

Table 2. PDCCH format and its size

Once an UE decodes the PDDCH, in the first 1-3 OFDM symbol of the first slot time of a subframe (a subframe consists of 2 slot time; the duration of a slot time is 0.5 ms) and finds that there is a DL assignment destined for it. This UE can decode the PDSCH, in the latter part of subframe to receive data. Hence, reception time for one DL assignment in the evaluation of this article is assumed to be 1 ms, a subframe time for a UE. We also assume that the eNB knows the wakeup time of UE according to DRX parameters, so there is no invalid PDCCH reception for UE. Since the reception time of an invalid PDCCH is very

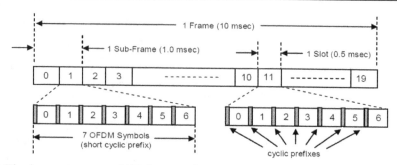

Fig. 17. The frame structure n LTE-A network.

short (1-3 OFDM time) and the possibility is very small, we ignore the energy to receive invalid PDCCHs in this chapter. Additionally, the UE must listen to the system information broadcast by eNB and send the Channel Quality Indicator (CQI) to eNB periodically, letting eNB have a good channel evaluation for resource scheduling and assignment. Furthermore, it must also send/receive ACK/NAK to/from eNB to indicate the correctness of previous receptions and transmissions. To simplify the evaluation in this chapter, the possible energies consumed listed above are ignored in this chapter.

3.3 The performances of DRX mechanism in LTE and LTE-A networks

3.3.1 Parameters in our proposed scheme

In order to meet the QoS requirement of real-time traffic such as VoIP and video, many constraints have to be obeyed. We list some energy consumptions in Equations (14)-(16)

$$D_e = (I_{DRX} - Dwakeup_t) \times D_p + Dwakeup_t \times Dwakeup_p \qquad (14)$$

$$L_e = (I_{DRX} - Lwakeup_t) \times L_p + Lwakeup_t \times Lwakeup_p \qquad (15)$$

$$I_e = I_{DRX} \times I_p \qquad (16)$$

The related parameters and their estimations are given in Table 3.

It is obvious that in order for UE to enter deep sleeping instead of light sleeping mode, the following conditions must be satisfied: $Dwakeup_t < I_{DRX}$, $D_e < I_e$, and $D_e < L_e$. We can get Equation (17) if the UE must be awake before the start of the next DRX cycle due to the QoS requirement of the traffic.

$$S_e = I_{DRX} \times (L_p - D_p) - (Lwakeup_t \times L_p - Dwakeup_t \times D_p) +$$
$$(Lwakeup_t \times Lwakeup_p - Dwakeup_t \times Dwakeup_p) > 0 \qquad (17)$$

If $S_e > 0$ is assumed so that the energy consumed in light sleeping mode is larger than that of deep sleeping mode, then

$$I_{DRX} > \frac{(Lwakeup_t \times L_p - Dwakeup_t \times D_p) + (Lwakeup_t \times Lwakeup_p - Dwakeup_t \times Dwakeup_p)}{(L_p - D_p)} > 0 \quad (18)$$

Parameter	Description	Estimation
TTI	Transmission Time Interval	1 ms
DRX_t	The duration of a DRX cycle in TTI	
$DRX_e(x)$	Energy consumed in a DRX cycle including a PDCCH message received in xth TTI of O-timer.	
$DRXL_e(x)$	Energy consumed in a DRX cycle when enters into light sleeping mode including a PDCCH message received in xth TTI of O-timer.	
P_e	Energy consumed in receiving a PDCCH message within a TTI (Estimation: 1 ms receiving time at estimated receiving power of 1 W)	1 mJ
O	O-Timer of a DRX cycle	$< DRX_t$
I	I-Timer of a DRX cycle	$< DRX_t$
I_{DRX}	The remaining period after the expiration of O-Timer in a DRX cycle	$= DRX_t{-}O$
D_p	The average power consumed when UE enters deep sleeping mode	10~50 mW
L_p	The average power consumed when UE enters light sleeping mode	80~160 mW
$Dwakeup_t$	The time needed for UE to wake up from deep sleeping mode to active mode	1~100 ms
$Lwakeup_t$	The time needed for UE to wake up from light sleeping mode to active mode	0.001~0.005 ms
$Dwakeup_p$	The average power consumed for UE to wake up from deep sleeping mode to active mode	0.5 ~1.5 W
$Lwakeup_p$	The average power consumed for UE to wake up from light sleeping mode to active mode	1~1.5 W
I_t	The remaining time for UE to remain in Inactive state after the expiration of I-Timer until the beginning of the next DRX cycle	
I_p	The average power consumed by UE in Inactive state.	400~700 mW
D_e	Energy consumed by UE during deep sleeping and in wake up from deep sleeping mode to active mode	
L_e	Energy consumed by UE during light sleeping and in wake up from light sleeping mode to active mode	
I_e	Energy consumed by UE in Inactive state until the beginning of the next DRX cycle	
S_e	The gap of the energy consumed by UE between entering light sleeping mode and deep sleeping mode during the interval from the expiration of I-Timer to the beginning of the next DRX cycle.	
$E_{efficiency}$	(The energy consumed by UE to receive one valid PDCCH message in a DRX cycle)/(The total energy consumed by UE in a DRX cycle)	< 1
$EL_{efficiency}$	(The energy consumed by UE to receive one valid PDCCH message in a DRX cycle)/(The total energy consumed by UE in a DRX cycle by entering light sleeping mode)	< 1

Table 3. Symbols and related parameters in the proposed methodology

Suppose D_p = 30 mW, L_p = 80 mW, $Dwakeup_p$ = 500 mW, $Lwakeup_p$ = 1300 mW, $Dwakeup_t$ = 50 ms, $Lwakeup_t$ = 0.003 ms, the condition to meet $S_e > 0$ is $I_{DRX} > 500$ ms. In other words, the duration from the expiration of I-Timer to the next DRX cycle must be at least 500 ms; otherwise the UE should enter light sleeping mode or not enter sleeping mode at all in order to reduce energy consumption. How can we decide whether UE should enter light sleeping mode or not if S_e is negative? The condition is that L_e must be less than I_e and $Lwakeup_t$ must be less than I_t. Since a DRX cycle is several TTIs in length, which is much longer than the time to wake up from light sleeping mode, the UE can enter light sleeping mode if $I_t > 0$. We devise an algorithm shown in Figure 18 to schedule the sleeping modes of UE based on the above analysis for delay-sensitive traffic.

001	wakeup at the beginning of a DRX cycle
002	DRX_timer ←DRX cycle
003	O_Timer ← O-Timer, I_Timer ← I-Timer
004	I_Falg ← False
005	While (DRX_timer > 0)
006	DRX_timer--
007	If DRX_timer <=0 then
008	Go to 001 /*Initiate another DRX cycle*/
009	End If
010	While ((O_Timer >0 and not L_Flag) or (I_Timer>0) and I_Flag)
011	If a PDCCH message is received then
012	I_Timer ← I_Timer-1
013	I_Flag ← true
014	End If
015	If DRX_Timer--<=0 then
016	Go to 001
017	End If
018	O_Timer ← O_Timer-1
019	If I_flag then
020	If I_Timer-- <=0 and O_timer<=0 then
021	Break
022	End If
023	End If
024	End While
025	If ((DRX_timer > 0) and (Se > 0)) then
026	Enter deep sleeping mode
027	Break
028	Else
029	Enter light sleeping mode
030	Break
031	End If
032	End While
031	Go to 001

Fig. 18. Sleeping mode scheduling of UE for delay-sensitive traffic in LTE network

The codes in line 001 to 003 stand for the beginning of a DRX cycle and DRX_timer, O_Timer and I_Timer are initiated by its respective timers. The I_Flag in line 004 used to indicate whether the I-Timer has been initiated or not. The while loop in line 005 stands for a DRX cycle loop and the DRX timer will be decreased by 1 when a TTI elapses shown in lines

006 and 015. If the DRX timer is expired as shown in lines 007 and 016, UE can initiate another DRX cycle. The **while** loop in line 010 monitors whether the O-Timer or I-Timer has been expired or not. The lines from 025 to 029 determine the S_e based on (6) is greater than 0 or not. If $S_e > 0$, the UE can enter into deep sleeping mode, else it must enter into light sleeping mode to save power consumption.

3.3.2 Evaluation environment

The traffic under evaluation is VoIP, following the G711 standard with 20 ms inter-packet arrival time. In order to meet the QoS requirement that the largest allowable delay is 20 ms, the UE must serve this traffic within one DRX cycle if we assume the length of a DRX cycle is also 20 ms. Note that silence suppression and bursty talks between two UEs are not considered in this study. Further assume that the probability of receiving a valid PDCCH message during an O-timer period is $f(x) = 1/(O)$ where x is in the range of 0 to $O-1$.

3.4 Performance results

3.4.1 Analysis

We can get the various kinds of energy consumed in one DRX cycle when a UE enters a deep sleeping mode instead of a light sleeping mode, as shown in the following Equations.

$$DRXL_e(x) = f(x)[P_e + (I_P(O-1) + I_P(I-(O-x-1)) + L_P(DRX_t - (I-O+x+1))) \times TTI] \quad (19)$$

$$\overline{DRXL}_e = \sum_{x=0}^{O-1} DRXL_e(x) = P_e + [I_P(I+O/2-1/2)) + L_P(DRX_t - (I-O/2+1/2))] \times TTI \quad (20)$$

$$DRX_e = (DRX_t - 1) \times I_P \times TTI + P_e \quad (21)$$

$$EL_{efficiency} = P_e / \overline{DRXL}_e \quad (22)$$

$$E_{efficiency} = P_e / DRX_e \quad (23)$$

$$E_{improve} = (DRX_e - \overline{DRXL}_e) / DRX_e \quad (24)$$

The meanings of the symbols in Equations (19)-(24) can be found in Table 2. The improved energy efficiency, $E_{improve}$ can refer Equation (24). In this study, we assume that the power in state of waiting for receiving a PDCCH is I_P, and the Round Trip Time (RTT) of Hybrid Automatic Repeat Request (HARQ) is ignored to simplify the computation. Assume that the parameters are the same as those used in the previous analysis, the energy efficiency of entering light sleeping mode $EL_{efficiency}$ and not entering sleeping mode $EL_{efficiency}$ is shown in Figure 19.

Figure 19 illustrates that the smaller the I-Timer, the higher the energy efficiency will be if a DRX cycle serves only one VoIP traffic with a 20 ms inter-arrival time. However, if the I-Timer is small, the delay for the real-time downlink traffic will be long. The eNB of LTE networks can decide what DRX parameters are to be applied based on the type of the served

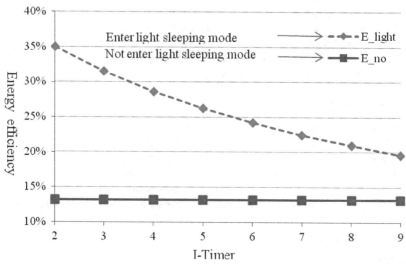

Fig. 19. Energy efficiency in a DRX cycle with VoIP traffic

traffic. The tradeoff between delay and energy efficiency is a critical factor in deciding whether to use the light sleeping mode or deep sleeping mode. We consider VoIP traffic with a Poisson distribution, $f(x) = e^{-\mu}\mu^x/x!$ where μ is the expected number of valid PDCCH messages in a DRX cycle and the parameters are the same as those used in the previous evaluation. We evaluate the energy consumption of UE and the delay when using light sleeping mode and deep sleeping mode, respectively. The delay and the energy consumption, denoted by D_L and E_L, can be expressed by Equations (25) and (25), respectively, when UE uses light sleeping mode to reduce energy consumption.

$$D_L = \sum_{x=0}^{\infty} f(x)D_l(x) = \sum_{x=0}^{\infty} \frac{e^{-\mu}\mu^x}{x!}D_l(x) \tag{25}$$

$$E_L = \sum_{x=0}^{\infty} f(x)E_l(x) = \sum_{x=0}^{\infty} \frac{e^{-\mu}\mu^x}{x!}E_l(x) \tag{26}$$

Here $D_L(x)$ and $E_L(x)$ stand for the delay and energy consumption when UE with the light sleeping scheme receives x PDCCH messages successfully. If we also assume the traffic received by eNB in the interval of a DRX cycle is random, the delay will depend on the time of reception within the DRX cycle. If the first PDCCH message of the traffic in the DRX cycle is received before O-Timer expires, the delay is near minimum, provided the propagation delay is ignored. Hence, the average delay of the traffic can be approximated by Equation (27).

$$D_l(x) = \begin{cases} \left(\sum_{t=0}^{DRX_t} t(\frac{1}{DRX_t})\right)\Big/x = \frac{(DRX_t+O)(DRX_t-O+1)}{2\,DRX_t x} & \text{if } x > 0 \\ \\ 0 & \text{if } x = 0 \end{cases} \tag{27}$$

As for $E_L(x)$, if x is greater than O-Timer, UE must wait for an additional I-Timer to see whether additional PDCCH messages will arrive. Therefore, $E_I(x)$ can be calculated by Equation (28).

$$E_I(x) = P_e x + (I_p I + L_p(DRX_t - (O + x + 1))) \times TTI + L_e \qquad (28)$$

If UEs save power consumption by entering deep sleeping mode, several DRX cycles may be needed for UEs to wake up from deep sleeping mode. In this situation, long DRX cycles must be used. One long DRX cycle is equivalent to several short DRX cycles. However, the delay will be much longer than that by entering light sleeping mode only. Under this circumstance, the number of short DRX cycles n must be greater than $\lceil Dwakeup_t/DRX_t \rceil$. The point is that n must be large enough so that the low sleeping power can compensate for the power consumed for the transition from sleeping mode to active mode. We give the delay, and energy consumed, for deep sleeping mode in Equations (29) and (30). We also assume that the $\overline{D_d(n)}$ average number of $\overline{E_d(n)}$ PDCCH messages received from eNB is 1 per short DRX cycle, the same as that in the evaluation of light sleeping mode.

$$\overline{D_d(n)} = (DRX_t - O + \sum_{i=1}^{n}(n-i)DRX_t)/n \ = \frac{n^2 - n + 2}{2n}DRX_t - O \qquad (29)$$

$$\overline{E_d(n)} = (nP_e + I_p I \times TTI + ((DRX_t - n - I + nDRX_t) \times TTI - Dwakeup_t) \times D_p + D_e)/n \qquad (30)$$

According to Equations (26), (30), (25), (29) and related parameters listed in Table 4, we get the energy consumed and the delay for each valid PDCCH message received as shown in Figures 20 and 21, respectively. Figure 21 shows that if UEs enter deep sleeping mode, the energy consumption (6.69 mJ) is still higher than that if UEs enter light sleeping mode (3.88 mJ) when the number of short DRX cycles is less than 10. However, when n increases above

Parameter	Value
I_p	400 mW
L_p	80 mW
TTI	1 ms
DRX_t	20 TTI
$Dwakeup_t$	50 ms
$Dwakeup_p$	500 mW
D_p	30 mW
D_e	25 mJ
O-Timer	2
I-Timer	4
Traffic	G711 VoIP
L_e	0.006 mJ

Table 4. Evaluation Parameters

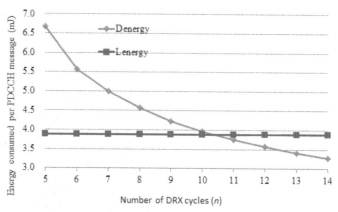

Fig. 20. Energy consumption vs. DRX cycles

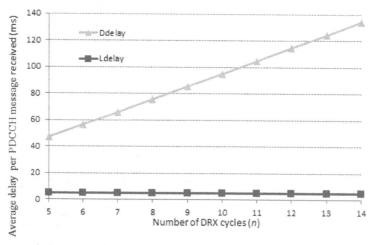

Fig. 21. Average delay as a function of DRX cycles

10, the energy consumption of UE entering deep sleeping mode will be lower than that of entering light sleeping mode, but as shown in Figure 21 the delay will increase from 42 *ms* to 130 *ms*.

4. Conclusion

The battery endurance is critical to the applications of mobile devices such as PDAs and smart phones. Simulations and analyses showed that if the number of active stations exceeds 16 and 128, the energy consumption can be reduced by over 57.2% and 72.7% respectively, i.e. the battery endurance for the 802.11 can be increased by a factor of two or more by applying this intelligent idle-listening scheme. Even if the number of stations is only one, the total energy consumption can be reduced by 21.7%. The scheme we proposed can be fully compatible with the legacy DCF and there will be no throughput reduction. The two-slot time strategy for space checking applied in the back-off is also a creative method.

Furthermore, the model of power analysis presented in this chapter based on Bianchi [13] is a good evaluation scheme for the power consumption to uplink a frame in MAC layer.

In this chapter, we also proposed a light sleeping mode applied in a short DRX cycle for the service of real time or QoS traffics. This study shows that both constraints of wakeup time and energy consumed arisen from deep sleeping mode inhibit the UE from entering into deep sleeping mode. The previous sections show that if the DRX timer is over about $200ms$ and the traffic can endure the delay up to $200ms$ ， the energy efficiency of entering into the deep sleeping mode is better than that of entering into the light sleeping mode. However, if the traffics of UE are very delay-sensitive, the huge transition overheads of waking up from deep sleeping mode prohibit the UE from entering into this mode. Hence, in this scenario entering into the light sleeping mode is the only selection to save power consumption and it can increase the power efficiency by 150%(=(35-14)/14x100%) compared with that of not entering into the any sleeping mode in DRX cycle if only one VoIP traffic is served in a DRX cycle. Our studies also show that if an UE wants to enter into the deep sleeping mode to reduce the power consumption instead of entering into the light sleeping mode, the period of the long DRX cycle must be over ten times of short DRX cycle with 20 TTIs so that it can gain energy efficiency, but at the cost of the delay increasing from $42ms$ to $140ms$. On the contrary, the delay of entering into the light sleeping mode is fixed at $3.88\ ms$ only.

5. Acknowledgment

The authors are deeply grateful for the help of the publishing process manager. With her help, we can print this chapter. Next, we want to thank National Science Council (NSC) for its grant project support in our study. With the support of grant projects of the co-authors, we can devote ourselves to the studies of LTE-A and 802.11.

6. References

[1] 3GPP TR 21.905: "3rd Generation Partnership Project; Technical Specification Group Services and System Aspects; Vocabulary for 3GPP Specifications," V11.0.1, Dec. 2011.

[2] 3GPP TS 36.211: "3rd Generation Partnership Project; Technical Specification Group Radio Access Network; Evolved Universal Terrestrial Radio Access (E-UTRA); Physical Channels and Modulation," V10.4.0, Dec. 2011.

[3] 3GPP TS 36.212: "3rd Generation Partnership Project; Technical Specification Group Radio Access Network; Evolved Universal Terrestrial Radio Access (E-UTRA); Multiplexing and channel coding," V10.4.0, Dec. 2011.

[4] 3GPP TS 36.213: "3rd Generation Partnership Project; Technical Specification Group Radio Access Network; Evolved Universal Terrestrial Radio Access (E-UTRA); Physical layer procedures," V10.4.0, Dec. 2011.

[5] 3GPP TS 36.307: "3rd Generation Partnership Project; Technical Specification Group Radio Access Network; Evolved Universal Terrestrial Radio Access (E-UTRA); Requirements on User Equipments (UEs) supporting a release-independent frequency band," V10.2.0, Sep. 2011.

[6] 3GPP TR 36.814, "Further advancements for E-UTRA physical layer aspects," v9.0.0 (Release 9), Mar. 2010.

[7] 3GPP TS 23.234, "Technical Specification Group Services and System Aspects; 3GPP System to Wireless Local Area Network (WLAN) Interworking; System Description," V10.3.0 (Release 10), Dec. 2011.

[8] 3GPP TS 25.304, "User Equipment (UE) procedures in idle mode and procedures for cell reselection in connected mode," V10.3.0 (Release 10), Dec. 2011.

[9] 3GPP TS 25.331, "Radio Resource Control (RRC) protocol specification," V11.0.0 (Release 11), Jan. 2012.

[10] 3GPP TS 36.300, "Evolved Universal Terrestrial Radio Access (EUTRA) and Evolved Universal Terrestrial Radio Access Network (EUTRAN); Overall description; Stage 2." V9.0.0 (Release 9), Dec. 2009.

[11] 3GPP TS 36.304, "E-UTRA: User Equipment Procedures in Idle Mode," Rel. 8, v. 8.2.0, May 2008.

[12] 3GPP TS 36.321, Evolved Universal Terrestrial Radio Access (EUTRA); Medium Access Control (MAC) protocol specification, V10.4.0 (Release 10), Dec. 2011.

[13] 3GPP TSG RAN WG2 meeting 57bis, R2-071285, DRX parameters in LTE-A, Mar. 2007.

[14] 3GPP, "3rd Generation Partnership Project; Technical Specification Group Radio Access Network; Evolved Universal Terrestrial Radio Access (E-UTRA) and Evolved Universal Terrestrial Radio Access Network (E-UTRAN); Overall description; Stage 2," Technical Specification 3GPP TS 36.300, v. 8.5.0, May 2009.

[15] 3GPP, "3rd Generation Partnership Project; Technical Specification Group Radio Access Network; Evolved Universal Terrestrial Radio Access (E-UTRA) Radio Resource Control (RRC); Protocol specification," Technical Specification 3GPP TS 36.331, v. 8.5.0, May 2009.

[16] 3rd Generation Partnership Project (3GPP); Requirements for Evolved UTRA (EUTRA) and Evolved UTRAN (E-UTRAN), http://www.3gpp.org/ftp/Specs/html-info/25913.htm.

[17] 3rd Generation Partnership Project (3GPP); Technical Specification Group Radio Access Network; Physical Layer Aspects for Evolved UTRA, http://www.3gpp.org/ftp/Specs/html-info/25814.htm.

[18] 3rd Generation Partnership Project; Technical Specification Group Radio Access Network; Physical Layer Aspects for Evolved Universal Terrestrial Radio Access (UTRA), 3GPP TR 25.814 V7.1.0, Sept. 2009.

[19] 3rd Generation Partnership Project; Technical Specification Group Radio Access Network; Evolved Universal Terrestrial Radio Access (E-UTRA); User Equipment (UE) radio transmission and reception (Release 8), 3GPP TS 36.101 v8.7.0, Sept. 2009.

[20] A. Saleh, "Frequency independent and frequency dependent nonlinear models of TWT amplifiers," *IEEE Transactions on Communications* 1981, 29(1), pp. 1715-1720.

[21] A.-K. Salkintzis and C. Chamzas, "*Performance Analysis of a Downlink MAC Protocol with Power-Saving Support*," *IEEE Transactions on Vehicular Technology, May* 2000, 49(3), pp. 1029-1040.

[22] K. Ahoi, J. Puttonen,T. Henttonen, and L. Dalsgaard, "Channel Quality Indicator Preamble for Discontinuous Reception," *Proc. Vehicular Technology Conference* 2010 (VTC 2010-Spring).

[23] B. Otal and J. Habetha, "Power saving efficiency of a novel packet aggregation scheme for high-throughput WLAN stations at different data rates," *Proc. Vehicular Technology Conference*, Vol. 3, pp. 2041–2045, , May/June 2005.

[24] L. Bononi, M. Conti, and L.Donatiello, "*A distributed contention control mechanism for power saving in random-access ad-hoc wireless local area networks*," Mobile Multimedia Communications, pp. 114–123, November 1999.

[25] C. Bontu and E. Illidge, "DRX Mechanism for Power Saving in LTE-A," *J. IEEE Communication Magazine*, 47, pp. 48-55, Jun. 2009.

[26] C. Ciochina, D. Mottier and H. Sari, "An Analysis of Three Multiple Access Techniques for the Uplink of Future Cellular Mobile Systems," *European Transactions on Telecommunications*, 19(5), pp. 58– 588, August 2008.

[27] CDPD Forum, Cellular Digital Packet Data System Specification: Release 1.1. Technical report, CDPD Forum, Inc., January 1995.

[28] *C.-H. Yeh, "Interference-aware Energy-efficient MAC Protocols for Sensor and Wireless Pervasive Networks," Proc. IEEE SMC, vol. 1, pp. 181–186, Oct. 8-11, 2006.*

[29] D. Jiang, H. Wang, E. Malkamki, and E. Tuomaala, "Principle and Performance of Semi-Persistent Scheduling for VoIP in LTE-A System," *Proc. International Conference on Wireless Communications, Networking and Mobile Computing* (WiCom'07), pp. 2861–2864, September 2007.

[30] D. Qiao and K.G. Shin, "Smart power-saving mode for IEEE 802.11 wireless LANs," *Proc. Annual Joint Conference of the IEEE Computer and Communications Societies (INFOCOM 2005)*, Miami, FL, March 13–17, 2005.

[31] Evaluation Methodology Document (EMD), IEEE Standard 802.16m-08/004r5, 2009.

[32] F. Boye, P. Rost, and G. Fettweis, "Adaptive radio resource management for a cellular system with fixed relay nodes," *Proc. IEEE Personal, Indoor and Mobile Radio Communications* (PIMRC'08), pp. 1–5, Sept. 2008.

[33] F.W Li, Y.Q. Zhang, L.W. Li, "Enhanced discontinuous reception mechanism for power saving in TD-LTE-A," *Proc. IEEE International Conference on Computer Science and Information Technology* (ICCSIT), 2010.

[34] G. Song and Y. Li, "Cross-layer Optimization for OFDMA Wireless Networks-Part II: Algorithm Development," *IEEE Wireless Communication*, 4, pp. 625–634, Mar. 2005.

[35] G. Bianchi, "*Performance Analysis of the IEEE 802.11 Distributed Coordination Function*," IEEE Journal On Selected Areas In Communications, Vol. 18, No. 3, March 2000.

[36] G. S. Kim, Y. H. Je, and S. Kim, "An adjustable power management for optimal power saving in LTE-A terminal baseband modem," *IEEE Transactions on Consumer Electronics*, 55(4), pp. 1847 – 1853, 2009.

[37] H. Ekström, A. Furusk"ar, J. Karlsson, M. Meyer, S. Parkvall, J. Torsner, and M. Wahlqvist, "Technical solutions for the 3G long term evolution," *IEEE Communications Magazine*, 44, pp. 38–45, March 2006.

[38] H. Holma and A. Toskala, *WCDMA for UMTS*, Third Ed., Wiley, 2004.

[39] H. Kaaranen, A. Ahtiainen, L. Laitinen, S. Naghian, and V. Niemi, *UMTS Networks*, Second Ed., Wiley, 2005.

[40] H. Sari, G. Karam, and I. Jeanclaude, "Transmission Techniques for Digital Terrestrial TV Broadcasting," *IEEE Communication. Magazine*, 33(2), pp. 100–109, Feb. 1995.

[41] H. Wu and T. Haustein, "Energy and Spectrum Efficient Transmission Modes for the 3GPP-LTE-A UL," *Proc. IEEE PIMRC*, pp. 1–5, Sept. 2007.

[42] H. Y. Lei, Performance Analysis of Power Management in WLAN and UMTS, PH.D. Thesis, North Carolina State University, 2005.

[43] B. Huang, H. Tian, L. Chen, and J. Zhu, "DRX-aware Scheduling Method for Delay-Sensitive Traffic," *IEEE Communications Letters*, 14(12), pp. 1113-1115, 2010.

[44] Chlamtac, Y. Fang, and H. Zeng, "Call Blocking Analysis for PCS Networks under General Cell Residence Time," *IEEE Wireless Communications and Networking Conference*, September 1999.

[45] *IEEE standard for Wireless LAN-Medium Access Control and Physical Layer Specification*, P802.11, November 1997.

[46] IEEE 802.11 WG, part 11a/11b/11g, *Wireless LAN Medium Access Control (MAC) and Physical Layer (PHY) specifications, Standard Specification, IEEE*, 1999.

[47] IEEE 802.11e, *Wireless LAN Medium Access Control (MAC) and Physical Layer (PHY) specification: Medium Access Control (MAC) Enhancements for Quality of Service (QoS)*, November 2005.

[48] IEEE P802.11n™/D3.0, "*Draft Amendment to STANDARD: Wireless LAN Medium Access Control (MAC) and Physical Layer (PHY) specifications: Enhancements for Higher Throughput*," Sept, 2007.

[49] J. Lim, H.G. Myung, and D.J. Goodman, "Proportional Fair Scheduling of Uplink Single-Carrier FDMA Systems," *Proc. 7th Annual IEEE International Symposium on Personal, Indoor and Mobile Radio Communications (PIMRC 06)*, Helsinki, Finland, Sept. 2006.

[50] J. Puttonen, T. Henttonen, N. Kolehmainen, K. Aschan, M. Moisio, and P. Kela, "Voice-over-IP Performance in UTRA Long Term Evolution Downlink," *Proc. IEEE Vehicular Technology Conference*, (VTC'S08), pp. 2502-2506, May 2008.

[51] J. Wiqard and T. Kolding, "On the User Performance of LTE-A UE Power Savings Schemes with Discontinuous Reception in LTE-A," *Proc. IEEE International Conference on Communications Workshops*, 2009.

[52] J.-H. Yeh et al., "Performance Analysis of Energy Consumption in 3GPP Networks," *Proc. Wireless Telecommun. Symp.*, pp. 67–72, May 2004.

[53] J. Snow, W.C. Feng, W.C. Feng, "Implementing a low power tdma protocol over 802.11," *Proc. WCNC*, pp. 75-80, 2005.

[54] R. Krashinsky and H. Balakrishnan, "Minimizing energy for wireless web access with bounded slowdown," *Wireless Network*, 11(1-2), pp. 135-148, 2005.

[55] K.C. Ting and F.P. Lai, "Design and Analysis of grouping-based DCF (GB-DCF) scheme for the MAC layer enhancement of 802.11 and 802.11n," *Proc. ACM/IEEE International Symposium on Modeling, Analysis and Simulation of Wireless and Mobile Systems*, 2006.

[56] K.C. Ting and F.P. Lai, "Design and Analysis of grouping-based DCF (GDCF) scheme for the MAC layer enhancement of 802.11," *Proc. Globecom*, 2006.

[57] K.C. Ting, F.C. Kuo, B.J. Hwang, H.C. Wang, and C.C. Tseng, "A Power-Saving and Robust Point Coordination Function for the transmission of VoIP over 802.11," *Proc. IEEE International Symposium on Parallel and Distributed Processing with Applications*, Taipei, Taiwan, September 6-9, 2010.

[58] K.C. Ting, F.C. Kuo, B.J. Hwang, H.C. Wang, and F.P. Lai, "An accurate power analysis model based on MAC layer for the DCF of 802.11n," *Proc. IEEE*

International Symposium on Parallel and Distributed Processing with Applications, Taipei, Taiwan, Sept. 6-9, 2010.

[59] K.C. Ting, H.C. Wang, C.C. Tseng, and F.C. Kuo, "Energy-Efficient DRX Scheduling for QoS Traffic in LTE Networks," *Proc. IEEE ISPA*, Busan, Korea, 26-28 May, 2011.

[60] L. Zhou, H.B. Xu and H. Tian, "Performance Analysis of Power Saving Mechanism with Adjustable DRX Cycles in 3GPP LTE-A," *Proc. IEEE 68th Vehicular Technology Conference* (VTC), IEEE Press, pp. 1-5, Oct. 2008.

[61] L.M. Feeney and M. Nilsson, "Investigating the Energy Consumption of a Wireless Network Interface in an Ad Hoc Networking Environment," *Proc. IEEE INFOCOM*, pp. 1548-1557, 2001.

[62] M. Anand, E. Nightingale, and J. Flinn, "Self-tuning wireless network power management," *Wireless Networks*, 11(4), pp. 451-469, Jul. 2005.

[63] M. Andrews, K. Kumaran, K. Ramanan, A. Stolyar, P. Whiting, and R. Vijayakumar, "Providing quality of service over a shared wireless link," *IEEE Communication Magazine*, 39(2), pp. 150-154, 2001.

[64] M. Keating, D. Flynn, R. Aitken, A. Gibbons, and K. Shi, *Low Power Methodology Manual*, Springer, 2007.

[65] Nokia, R2-071285, *DRX parameters in LTE*, March 2007

[66] P. Kela, J. Puttonen, N. Kolehmainen, T. Ristaniemi, T. Henttonen, and M. Moisio, "Dynamic Packet Scheduling Performance in UTRA Long Term Evolution Downlink," *Proc. International Symposium on Wireless Pervasive Computing (ISWPC)*, May 2008.

[67] X. Perez-Costa and D. Camps-Mur, "APSM: bounding the downlink delay for 802.11 power save mode," *Proc. IEEE International Conference on Communications* (ICC 05), pp. 3616–3622, 2005.

[68] R. Dinis, D. Falconer, C.T. Lam, and M. Sabbaghian, "A Multiple Access Scheme for the Uplink of Broadband Wireless Systems," *Proc. IEEE GLOBECOM, Dec.* 2004 (Dallas, TX), 6, pp. 3808–3812.

[69] R. Schoenen, R. Halfmann, and B. H. Walke, "MAC performance of a 3GPP-LTE-A multihop cellular network", *Proc. IEEE Int. Conf. Communications (ICC'08)*, pp. 4819–4824, May 2008.

[70] R. van Nee and R. Prasad, OFDM for Wireless Multimedia Communications, Artech House, 2000.

[71] S. Nath, Z. Anderson, and S. Seshan, "Choosing beacon periods to improve response times for wireless HTTP clients," *Proc. ACM International Workshop on Mobility Management and Wireless Access*, pp. 43-50, Philadelphia, PA, Sept. 26-Oct. 1, 2004.

[72] S.R. Yang and Y.B. Lin, "Modeling UMTS Discontinuous Reception Mechanism," *IEEE Transactions on Wireless Communications*, vol. 4, pp. 312-319, Jan. 2005.

[73] S.R. Yang, "Dynamic Power Saving Mechanism for 3G UMTS System," *J. Mobile Networks and Applications*, 2, pp. 5-14, Jan. 2007.

[74] S.R. Yang, S.Y. Yan, and H.N. Hung, "Modeling UMTS Power Saving with Bursty Packet Data Traffic," *J. IEEE Transactions on Mobile Computing*, 6, pp. 1398-1409, Dec. 2007.

[75] S. Yang, M. Yoo, and Y. Shin, "An Adaptive Discontinuous Reception Mechanism Based on Extended Paging Indicator for Power Saving in UMTS," *Proc. IEEE 64th Vehicular Technology Conference (VTC)*, pp. 1-5, Sept. 2006.

[76] S.J. Kwon, Y.W. Chung, and D.K. Sung, "Queueing Model of Sleep- Mode Operation in Cellular Digital Packet Data," *IEEE Transactions on Vehicular Technology*, 52(4), pp. 1158–1162, July 2003.

[77] T. Kolding, J. Wigard, and L. Dalsgaard, "Balancing Power Saving and Single User Experience with Discontinuous Reception in LTE-A," *Proc. IEEE International Symposium on Wireless Communication Systems* (ISWCS'08), October 2008.

[78] T. Takiguchi, S. Saruwatari, T. Morito, S. Ishida, M. Minami, and H. Morikawa, "A Novel Wireless Wake-Up Mechanism for Energy-Efficient Ubiquitous Networks," *Proc. IEEE Communications Conferences*, pp. 1–5, 2009.

[79] K.C. Ting, H.C. Lee, H.H. Lee, and F.P. Lai, "An idle listening-aware energy efficient scheme for the DCF of 802.11n," *IEEE Transactions on Consumer Electronics*, 55(2), pp. 447–454, 2009.

[80] Texas Instrument, http://www.cse.ohio-state.edu/siefast/nest/nest_webpage/datasheet/Chipcon%20-%20CC1000%20Data%20Sheet%20v2.1.pdf, Chipcon AS SmartRF, CC1000 Preliminary Datasheet (rev. 2.1), April 19, 2002.

[81] X. Wang, J. Yin, and D.P. Agrawal, "Analysis and optimization of the energy efficiency in the 802.11 DCF," *Journal of Mobile Networks and Applications*, 11(2), pp. 279–286, 2006.

[82] Winspring Wireless Technologies, WS9901 2.4GHz ISM Band Linear Power Amplifier, WS9901spec.pdf.

[83] Y. Sun, S. Du, O. Gurewitz, and D.B. Johnson, "DW-MAC: A Low Latency, Energy Efficient Demand-Wakeup MAC Protocol for Wireless Sensor Networks," *Proc. MobiHoc'08*, Hong Kong, China, May 26–30, 2008.

[84] W. Ye, J. Heidemann, and D. Estrin, "An energy-efficient MAC protocol for wireless sensor networks," *Proc. IEEE INFOCOM*, pp. 1567-1576, 2002.

[85] C.H. Yeh, "Interference-Aware energy-efficient MAC protocols for sensor and wireless pervasive networks," *Proc. IEEE International Conference on Systems, Man and Cybernetics*, pp. 181-186, 2006.

[86] Z. Zhou, X. Xiang, X. Wang, and J. Pan, "An energy-efficient data-dissemination protocol in wireless sensor networks," *Proc. International Symposium on a World of Wireless, Mobile and Multimedia Networks*, pp. 10-22, 2006.

Energy Efficiency of Connected Mobile Platforms in Presence of Background Traffic

Sameh Gobriel, Christian Maciocco and Tsung-Yuan Charlie Tai
Circuits and Systems Research Lab, Intel Labs, Intel Corporation
USA

1. Introduction

In the last decade there has been an explosive growth in popularity of mobile computing platforms which include laptops, notebooks, tablets, cell phones, etc. However, the usability of these devices from end users point of view is directly associated with their battery life and the fact that they are powered by non-continuous energy sources imposes a serious limitations to these devices. As a result, a typical architecture design of such mobile computing platforms will include low power platform states for individual components (e.g. CPU, memory controller, hard-disk, etc.) or for the whole platform. These low power states can be *sleep* states where the components or the whole platform is in a non-operational mode (e.g. operating systems defined sleep states: standby, hibernate, etc.) or *scaled* states where they are operating at lower than peak performance (e.g. CPU dynamic voltage and frequency scaling (DVFS)). For example the Advanced Configuration and Power Interface (ACPI) specifies power management concepts and interfaces. ACPI integrates the operating system, device drivers, system hardware components, and applications for power management and defines several power states for each component ranging from fully powered on to fully powered-off with each successive state consuming the same or less amount of power.

Individual power management techniques differ in (1) how deep the low power state is, where usually a deeper sleep state has a higher exit latency and hence a negative performance impact, (2) the algorithms used to manage entering and exiting these low power states and (3) optimizations to extend these sleep states as long as possible so additional system components having longer exit latency could also be put into lower power state. Standard policies are usually based on *timeout* approaches, where the platform or individual components are transitioned in low-power modes if they have been observed "idle" for the duration of a timeout. Usually this timeout value is dynamic and depends on the current operating state and the previous history of idle and active platform states.

Recent measurements and field assessments have shown that: in offices, desktop systems at a minimum remain powered up all day long whether being actively used or not, and further, two-thirds of such systems are fully on after work hours, with only 4% operating in sleep modes. It appears plausible that network connectivity drives much of this and these systems remain available to facilitate sporadic, occasional activity, such as user remote access, administrator access for maintenance, etc. (backups, patch management). On the other hand, in the residential sector, the average PC is on 34% of the time and spends only 4% of the time in an some form of sleep state and more than half the time a PC is on no one is actively using the machine.

In this chapter we will argue that a major hurdle for end systems desiring to enter a sleep state arises from the network and the desire of end users to stay *"always on and always connected"* to the network. We first focus on powered-on platforms but idle (i.e. not running an active heavy workload) and quantify the effect of background network traffic on the platform energy-efficiency. then, we propose a low-overhead mitigation techniques that can detect and classify network traffic with no dependencies on network protocols nor the platform and present simulation analysis of these techniques and algorithms based on live network traces. Finally we describe our firmware based implementation in our prototype Wireless Network Interface Cards (WNIC) and show our practical results when applied in live networks.

2. Related work

Several mechanisms have been proposed to reduce the energy consumption of networked platforms. Prior work can largely be grouped in three categories: reducing the active power consumption of systems when they are awake Agarwal et al. (2008); Flinn & Satyanarayanan (2004); Li et al. (2007), reducing the power consumption of the network infrastructure, routers and switches Gunaratne et al. (2005); Gupta & Singh (2003); Nedevschi et al. (2008) and opportunistically putting the devices to sleep Agarawal et al. (2009); Shih et al. (2002); Sorber et al. (2005). *Long Idle* falls in the third category, where it advocates for localized energy-efficient optimization within the platform to extend the sleeping state of the platform rather than using a network-wide implementation of a proxy (wakeup) service. However, in contrast with previous work *Long idle* did not assume a special magic packet for wake-on WLan (WoWLAN) Shih et al. (2002) nor it uses multiple network interface cards Sorber et al. (2005), and it did not assume any application level optimization to offload background traffic processing Agarawal et al. (2009). *Long idle* requires only a single network interface card and detects background traffic without the need to decrypt the data payload by gathering traffic statistics (size, direction, interarrival time, etc.) on the ongoing communication. In this chapter, we show that such non intrusive technique achieves a good detection accuracy and extends the platform sleeping state with no need for a more sophisticated technique or a special hardware.

3. Problem formulation

In this section, we analyze and quantify the negative impact of continuously interrupting the platform to process the background and management network traffic and highlight the effect on the platform energy-efficiency.

3.1 Platform PM energy gain

Current platform power management guides the platform to enter a lower power state (sleeping state Sx) if it detects a period of idleness; τ_{idle}. The more the system stays in sleep state un-interrupted the better the energy gain is, because more and more peripherals can enter a low power state and/or because deeper sleep states with longer exit latency can be used.

Recent work has shown that Smart timing approaches for Operating systems (OS) can be used to increase the quiet times for the OS by skipping timer tick interrupts when the platform is idle or by adaptively changing the rate of timer interrupts (e.g., Olsen & Narayanaswami (2006)) which form the basis for *"tickless OS"* where the OS is moving away from scheduling periodic clock interrupts every few milliseconds to a more event-driven approach Gleixner & Molnar (2006); Yodaiken & Barabanov (1997) where the OS is waken to process an event being posted by the applications or by the hardware on demand.

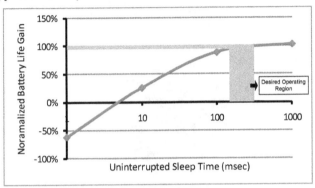

Fig. 1. Typical Platform PM Energy Gain

Figure 1 represents the energy gain of platform power management and typically the achieved gain follows a non-decreasing concave reward function Olsen & Narayanaswami (2006); Siddha et al. (2007). The x-axis represents the break event time, i.e., guaranteed platform quietness period, and the y-axis represents the normalized increase in the total battery life when the system enters a low power state normalized to the case when it remains in the same fully active state (S0). The desired operating range is highlighted and extending the sleeping time beyond the highlighted range has a diminishing return in the energy gain as it is not possible to extend the tick rate for the OS beyond the highlighted range Olsen & Narayanaswami (2006) and the system will be wakened for some scheduled event at about this range.

3.2 Background traffic effect on platform PM

When a system is connected to a network, even when the user is not engaged in any active communication the system engages in what we term "background/noise" traffic. These packets can be network maintenance or management packets (e.g., ARP, DHCP, etc.), network services handshake (e.g., directory services, NetBIOS) or application heartbeats (e.g., Instant Messaging, Windows Widgets, etc.). Figures 2 and 3 show the average and variance in the number of network packets processed per second and the protocol mix of two examples of this background traffic. Figure 2 is a wired network trace for a home environment and Figure 3 is a wireless trace for a platform connected to an enterprise network.

It should be clear that these network traces are shown here as examples of real-life networks and cannot be generalized as the default background traffic in these networks. As previously mentioned the traffic characteristics will be remarkably different from location to location based on the network infrastructure architecture, platforms and applications used, number of network users, time of data collection etc. In fact chattier and less chatty background

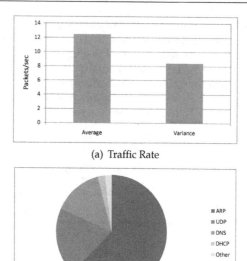

(a) Traffic Rate

(b) Protocol Mix

Fig. 2. Home Wired Network Background Traffic

and management network traffic has been reported in different literatures Gunaratne et al. (2005). One of the significance of our work is that it is not designed to target specific network conditions and no specific background/management traffic network optimization (e.g., ARP-Proxy Nedevschi et al. (2009), Network Proxy Offload *TC38-TG4 Proxying support for sleep modes Specifications* (2009), etc.) is assumed.

For a networked platform keeping the sleep state of the system uninterrupted is a challenge. Network activity will interrupt the sleeping state because the host is waken-up to process these packets. Moreover, each time the sleeping state is interrupted the platform will have to wait for the timeout (i.e., τ_{idle}) before re-entering the low power state.

It should be noted however, that τ_{idle} can't be a small value because this will have a negative impact on active workload due to the overhead (entry and exit latency and power overhead) associated with transitioning to and from the low power managed state. For example if a Wireless NIC is used and according to the 802.11 Power Saving Mode (PSM) *IEEE 802.11, Part 11: Wireless LAN Medium Access Control (MAC) and Physical Layer (PHY) Specifications* (1999) each time the NIC enters the sleep mode, it has to wait for the next beacon advertised by the base station before it can receive any of its buffered packets in the base station. Typically the beacon interval is set at 100 msec which means that the exit latency from the sleep state of the wireless NIC in PSM is 100 msec. Hence, if the sleep state is entered blindly each time there is packet-free time the active communication performance (e.g., throughput, latency, etc.) will significantly degrade.

The net effect of background traffic can be viewed as depicted in Figure 4 (dotted red line). If the interpacket arrival time is X msec then longer platform sleep times are not available and thus the energy gain of platform power management beyond some value is not achievable.

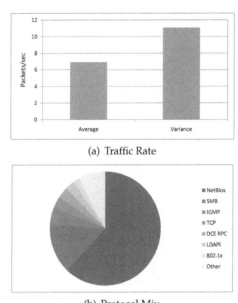

(a) Traffic Rate

(b) Protocol Mix

Fig. 3. Enterprise Wireless Network Background Traffic

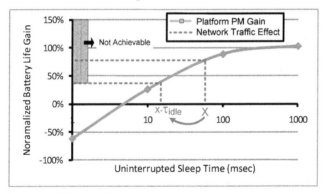

Fig. 4. Traffic Effect on PM Energy Gain

Moreover, encountering an additional performance guard timeout before re-entering the low power state will degrade the net energy gain of platform power management even further (for illustration $\tau_{idle} = 50$ msec in figure).

Figure 5(a) plots the Cumulative distribution function of uninterrupted packet free times in different environments. As shown in figure in an enterprise environment (traffic trace example shown in Figure 3) almost 40% of the time the platform will be hit by a packet within 100 msec and in a wired home environment (traffic trace example shown in Figure 2) the probability is about 60%. The platform power management energy gain degrades accordingly with background network traffic. If we assume that the platform activities are synchronized and an uninterrupted sleep time of 100 msec is guaranteed each time the platform enters

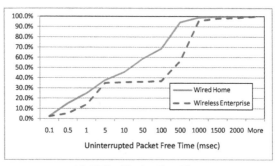

(a) CDF of Packet Free Time

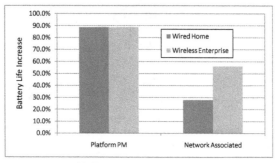

(b) Energy Gain @ 100 msec

Fig. 5. Platform PM Gain With Network Traffic

the sleep state then battery life is extended by almost 88%. On the other hand when the platform is associated with the network and is processing the background network traffic the gain diminishes (even with $\tau_{idle} = 0$ msec) to only 56% for the example wireless enterprise network and to about 27% for the wired home environment as shown in Figure 5(b)

3.3 Background traffic processing cost

We use Windows Performance Tools (WPT) Kit *Windows Performance Analysis Tools* (2008) designed for measuring and analyzing system and application performance on Windows to quantify the processing cost of each packet of background traffic at the different layers of the networking stack and to highlight that each packet will generate at least one interrupt which will wake the platform up to exit the low power platform state.

Figure 6(a) plots the processing cost of Layer 2 (L2) packets. It shows the interrupts and the Deferred Procedure Calls (DPC) generated by the NIC when L2 packets are processed. As shown in the figure when beacons are received the NIC generates two interrupts reflecting information (TIM info, SNR data, etc.) being DMA-ed into the host memory these two interrupts are spaced within approximately 0.5 msec. Each interrupt is followed by a DPC reflecting that the NIC driver is running. Investigating the shape and reasons of these interrupts is beyond the scope of this chapter but we highlight that for each of these interrupts or the DPC the CPU is running (C0 at 800 MHz) indicating that host is wakened up to process each of them.

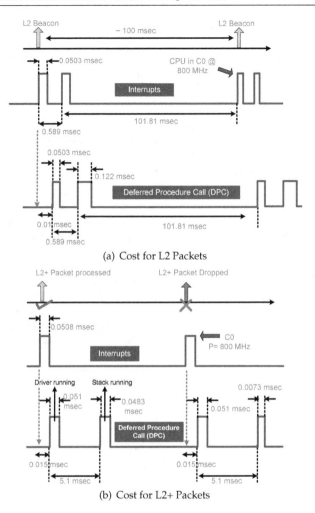

(a) Cost for L2 Packets

(b) Cost for L2+ Packets

Fig. 6. Processing Cost for Background Packets

Figure 6(b) plots the processing cost of L2+ packets (all the packets that are traced in Figures 2 and 3). As shown in figure each of the L2+ packets cause an interrupt reflecting a memory DMA for the packet data followed by two DPCs one is caused by the NIC driver running and the other by the TCP/IP OS stack running. The running time of each depends on whether the packet is dropped or is processed but similarly what we want to highlight is that the host is interrupted at least once to process each of these packets.

4. Long Idle technology

We define an architecture and a low-overhead technique, which we call *Long Idle* to enable the NIC to classify incoming packets into active versus background traffic and intelligently hold the background traffic on the NIC device to guarantee idleness so that the system can enter low power states with no impact on performance. It should be noted, however, that although we present *Long Idle* technology as something that we implemented in the NIC there is nothing that prevents the network designer from applying that same technique into for example, network switches and/or network wireless access points.

4.1 Long Idle overview

By definition background packets are not for active communication, hence, typically these packets are not time critical and can be delayed for extended period of time without any impact on the user experience. In fact most of these background packets are discarded by the host after processing them Nedevschi et al. (2009; 2008).

Unfortunately, at the NIC level it is not possible (without performing deep inspection of the packet) to know whether the packet will be of any use to the host or not. Since for all practical reasons the time and processing overhead and energy of deep packet inspection is intolerable at that NIC level if at all possible due security and encryption (e.g., VPN, etc.), the hypothesis of *Long Idle* is: if the NIC can classify the incoming packets into active versus background traffic without having to look inside the packet then the NIC can intentionally buffer the background packets and guarantee uninterrupted quietness to the platform for extended amount of time, e.g., few hundreds msec, and then send these packets as one burst to the host for processing. Figure 7 depicts the *Long Idle* concept. Moreover, since the created quietness period is guaranteed not to be interrupted except for active traffic then the platform can *instantly* enter a sleep state for the whole duration of the buffering period (without waiting for τ_{idle}) to save its energy even further.

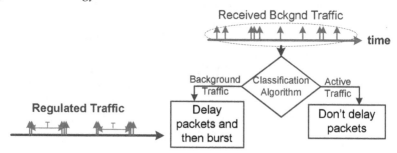

Fig. 7. Long Idle Overview

4.2 Long Idle algorithm

Once a packet is received at the NIC and is classified as belonging to background traffic the packet is not instantly pushed to the host, but instead buffered inside the NIC's internal memory until one of few events occurs: Either, a *Long Idle* timeout event has occurred (maximum time watermark (e.g., 300 msec) for holding a background packet is reached) or a packet belonging to an active communication is received in the Rx FIFO or the Rx FIFO has reached some occupancy threshold (maximum bytes to hold for background traffic).

Long Idle relies on the NIC's ability to differentiate the active traffic from the idle background one without a need for packet deep inspection. Based on our analysis the main differences in the traffic patterns can be summarized as follows:

1. Idle traffic is mostly small-sized packets (typically a heartbeat or a management packet is only few tens of bytes) and MTU size packets are rarely seen in idle traffic.

2. Because most of the management and background traffic is transmitted by the network, idle traffic is mostly on the receive path.

3. Active small-sized packets (e.g., those belong to a VoIP or a gaming session) are mostly two-way communication.

4. A large percentage of the Idle traffic is broadcast packets, while active communication is mostly sending and receiving unicast packets.

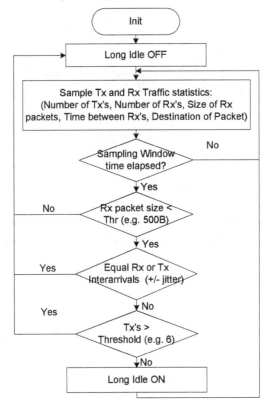

Fig. 8. Long Idle Sampling State Machine

Our algorithm for enabling *Long Idle* is composed of two state machines. One is continuously sampling the ongoing traffic and classifies whether it is active versus background at the end of the sampling window and is independent from the NIC used (wired or wireless), the other is defining how to handle the packet based on the classification result and clearly this depends on the type of the NIC used. In this chapter, we use the Wireless NIC as an example and show how the packet handling can be coupled with 802.11 PSM u-apsd *IEEE 802.11, Part 11: Wireless LAN Medium Access Control (MAC) and Physical Layer (PHY) Specifications* (1999) mode.

As shown in Figure 8, the algorithm for traffic sampling and *Long Idle* divides the time into slices of sampling windows. During this sampling window statistics on the size,

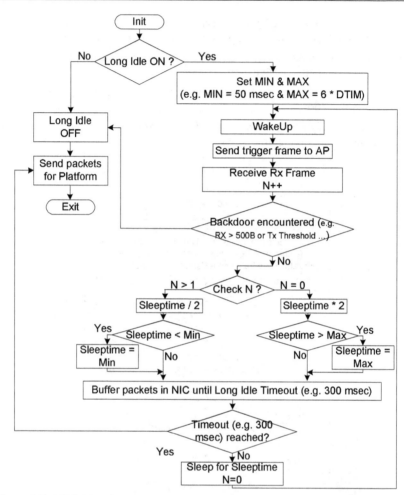

Fig. 9. Long Idle WNIC Implementation

destination, interarrival times, and number of transmitted and received packets are collected and based on the conditions outlined above the ongoing communication is classified as active versus background one. Figure 9 depicts the wireless NIC sleep time update based on the classification of the ongoing traffic. If *Long Idle* is detected the Wireless NIC sleeps longer and the received packet is buffered for extended amount of time. On the other hand, as soon as the NIC receives a packet that it classifies as belonging to an active communication the *Long Idle* mode is set to off and these packets are pushed to the platform instantly.

5. Evaluation and analysis

In our analysis we evaluate the performance of the *Long idle* technology. First we quantify its traffic classification accuracy and then we evaluate the power and performance impact in case of both idle and active workloads with and without using *Long idle*.

5.1 Traffic categorization accuracy

Long Idle relies on the NIC's ability to categorize the network traffic based on the conditions and algorithms outlined in Section 4. We use real-network traffic traces (as mentioned in Section 3) that represent hours of idle and active platform network activities as an input to our *Long idle* simulator running the classification and traffic-type-specific data handling algorithms to quantify the accuracy of these algorithms.

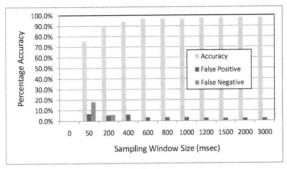

(a) Wired Environment

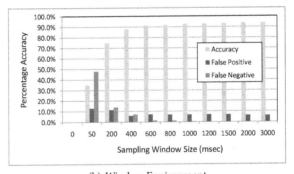

(b) Wireless Environment

Fig. 10. Long Idle Classification Algorithm Accuracy

Figure 10 analyzes the accuracy of the traffic classification algorithm in two environments wired home environment and wireless enterprise environment. The trend of this result is the same for all other tested networks. The false positive ratio represents the percentage of time idle traffic has been classified as active (i.e., the platform is waken up unnecessarily to process these idle packets) to the total time until it is correctly classified as idle. The false negative ratio represents the percentage of time active traffic is classified as idle (i.e., packets are held in the NIC and processing is delayed).

Figure 10 illustrates the effectiveness of our traffic categorization algorithm. As shown in the figure the average accuracy of the algorithm at a sampling window size of 1 sec in an enterprise environment is about 92% and in a home environment is close to 96%. The false negative percentage is very small which indicates that active traffic is never classified as idle, as a result active traffic is not buffered in the NIC and hence the active traffic performance and the user experience are unaffected. As shown in the figure most of the classification errors are false positives (idle classified as active) which indicates that a small percentage of the power reduction opportunities have been missed and the platform is waken up unnecessarily.We confirm these simulations with implementation results presented in the next subsections.As expected the classification accuracy improves with increasing the sampling window but, on the other hand, the response time defined as how fast the platform will react to traffic changes degrades. As shown in the figure the classification accuracy saturates mostly at a sampling window size of 700 msec. Based on our results a sampling window size of 1 sec achieves a good classification accuracy and good responsiveness with unaffected user experience.

5.2 Idle traffic impact

We implemented *Long Idle* classification algorithm in a prototype Intel WiFi 5350 NIC *Intel WiFi Link 5100 Series Specifications* (2008). In our implementation we used a sampling window size of 1 sec and NIC idle traffic buffering timeout of 300 msec.

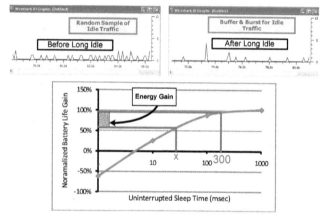

Fig. 11. Implementation Impact on Idle Traffic

Figure 11 plots the behavior of the NIC with idle traffic. Whenever the platform is not engaged in an active communication *Long Idle* technology will guarantee a quietness period as large as the buffering timeout value (e.g., 300 msec) set in the NIC and therefore the platform will stay in a low-power state uninterrupted during this time. Compared to Figure 5(b), energy gain achieved by Long Idle is about 23% for wireless environment and about 41% for the wired environment. It should be noted that we assumed that $\tau_{idle} = 0$ (see Section 3) to report worst case benefit and any value for $\tau_{idle} > 0$ will increase the energy gain of *Long Idle* even further.

5.3 Active traffic impact

To quantify the effect of *Long Idle* on active workloads we used our NIC prototype implementation to run various NetIQ Chariot *NetIQ Chariot 4.0 testing tools* (2001) benchmarks. NetIQ Chariot is a prepackaged real-world benchmarking tool widely used for network performance evaluation. We present results for FTP throughput and VoIP Mean Opinion Score (MOS) tests.

Table 1 represents the network throughput achieved by the NIC with and without *Long Idle* compared to the traditional 80.11 PSM. As shown in the table, the network throughout is

Input Rate	802.11 Observed Rate	Long Idle Observed Rate
256 Kbps	256 Kbps	256 Kbps
512 Kbps	512 Kbps	512 Kbps
1 Mbps	0.995 Mbps	0.985 Mbps
2 Mbps	1.997 Mbps	1.964 Mbps
10 Mbps	9.875 Mbps	9.7656 Mbps

Table 1. FTP Throughput with Long Idle

not degraded when *Long Idle* is used which indicates that the NIC correctly classified the FTP session as an active communication session and backed off from buffering any network packets. The slight difference in throughput between 802.11 PSM and that achieved by *Long Idle* is because *long Idle* has a slower responsiveness, as mentioned in Section 5.1, and the "first" packet in an active communication is delayed until at least one sampling window (i.e., 1 sec) has elapsed before the ongoing traffic is classified as active.

VoIP Session	802.11 PSM Quality	Long Idle Quality
Two Way	4.37	4.34
	4.37	4.37
One Way	4.37	4.33

Table 2. VoIP Quality with Long Idle

VoIP MOS is a numerical method of expressing voice and video quality it is a measurable indication of the perceived quality of the media received after being transmitted and eventually compressed using codecs. A MOS value larger than 4.0 is what VOIP services targets as a good quality VoIP session *ITU-T Rec. G.729 Annex B, A silence compression scheme for G.729 optimized for terminals conforming to Rec. V.70* (1996). Table 2 represents the MOS results achieved by the NIC with and without *Long Idle*. Similarly, when *Long Idle* is enabled it correctly identifies the active communication and the packets are not buffered in NIC and hence no user experience impact. Similar to the FTP case, the small difference in the MOS score is attributed to the delay experienced by the first packet.

6. Conclusion

Typical platform power management relies on guiding individual platform components or the whole platform into low energy *(sleep)* states when the platform has been observed "idle" for some time with no active workloads. Individual power management techniques differ in how deep the sleep state is, the algorithms used to enter and exit the sleep states and optimizations to extend these sleep states as long as possible. In this chapter, we showed that significant energy is wasted at the platform level while it is idle and connected to a network because the system is processing background and management traffic. We showed that these background packets arrive at a rate high enough that can prevent the system from taking full advantage of the platform-level power management states. We quantified the negative impact of network connectivity on platform energy-efficiency and showed.

We proposed *Long Idle* a low overhead technique that is implemented inside the network interface card with no dependency from the host, application or the network infrastructure to classify the ongoing traffic into active versus background without deep packet inspection and to locally buffer the background traffic in the NIC to guarantee uninterrupted sleep periods for the platform. We showed that when our scheme is used the total platform sleep time increases by up to 40% with no performance degradation and no user experience impact.

7. References

Agarawal, Y., Hodges, S., Chandra, R., Scott, J., Bahl, P. & Gupta, R. (2009). Somniloquy: Augmenting network interfaces to reduce pc energy usage, *USENIX Symposium on Networked Systems Design and Implementation (NSDI)*.

Agarwal, Y., Pering, T., Want, R. & Gupta, R. (2008). SwitchR: reducing system power consumption in multi-clients multi radio environment, *IEEE International Symposium on Wearable Computers (ISWC)*.

Flinn, J. & Satyanarayanan, M. (2004). Managing battery lifetime with energy aware adaptation, *ACM Transactions on Computer Systems*.

Gleixner, T. & Molnar, I. (2006). Dynamic ticks, http://lwn.net/Articles/202319/.

Gunaratne, C., Christensen, K. & Nordman, B. (2005). Managing energy consumption costs in desktop pcs and lan switching with proxying, split tcp connections and scaling of link speed, *International Journal of Network Management*.

Gupta, M. & Singh, S. (2003). Greening of the internet, *ACM Sigcomm*.

IEEE 802.11, Part 11: Wireless LAN Medium Access Control (MAC) and Physical Layer (PHY) Specifications (1999). IEEE.

Intel WiFi Link 5100 Series Specifications (2008). www.intel.com.

ITU-T Rec. G.729 Annex B, A silence compression scheme for G.729 optimized for terminals conforming to Rec. V.70 (1996).

Li, X., Gupta, R., Adve, S. & Zhou, Y. (2007). Cross component energy management: Joint adaptation of processor and memory, *ACM Transactions on Architure and Code Optimization*.

Nedevschi, S., Chandrashekar, J., Liu, J., Nordman, B., , Ratnasamy, S. & Taft, N. (2009). Skilled in the art of being idle: Reducing energy waste in networked systems, *USENIX Symposium on Networked Systems Design and Implementation (NSDI)*.

Nedevschi, S., Popa, L., Iannaccone, G., Ratnasamy, S. & Wetherall, D. (2008). Reducing network energy consumption via sleeping and rate adaptation, *USENIX Symposium on Networked Systems Design and Implementation (NSDI)*.

NetIQ Chariot 4.0 testing tools (2001). http://www.netiq.com.

Olsen, C. & Narayanaswami, C. (2006). PowerNap: An efficient power management scheme for mobile devices, *IEEE Transactions on Mobile Computing*.

Shih, E., Bahl, P. & Sinclair, M. (2002). Wake on wireless: An event driven energy saving strategy for battery operated devices, *IEEE International Conference on Mobile Computing and Networking (MobiCom)*.

Siddha, S., Pallipadi, V. & Ven, A. V. D. (2007). Getting maximum mileage out of tickless, *Linux Symposium Proceedings*.

Sorber, J., Banerjee, N., Corner, M. & Rollins, S. (2005). Turducken: Hierarchical power management for mobile devices, *IEEE International Conference on Mobile Systems, Applications and Services (MobiSys)*.

TC38-TG4 Proxying support for sleep modes Specifications (2009). http://www.acpi.info/.

Windows Performance Analysis Tools (2008). http://msdn.microsoft.com/en-us/performance/.

Yodaiken, V. & Barabanov, M. (1997). A real-time linux, *Linux Journal*.

Monitoring Energy Efficiency in Buildings with Wireless Sensor Networks: *NRG-WiSe Building*

I. Foche, M. Chidean, F.J. Simó-Reigadas, I. Mora-Jiménez,
J.L. Rojo-Álvarez, J. Ramiro-Bargueno and A.J. Caamano*

Signal Theory and Communications Dept., ETSIT, Rey Juan Carlos University, Madrid, Spain

1. Introduction

Over the last decades the economic growth has steadily increased the demand for energy, but "without a change in policy, the world is on a path for a rise in global temperature of up to 6⁰ C, with catastrophic consequences for our climate" International Energy Agency (2009). This is an important issue presented in the *World Energy Outlook 2009* of the International Energy Agency (IEA) in which are treated a lot of reasons leading global energy development is unsustainable. This mentioned change in policy implies a world wide common position and a very high economic cost which will be offset by health and energy-security benefits, so *it is worth the economic cost*. For that reason in this regard have been made some efforts.

At present, the economic and financial crisis is producing the first fall in the global energy use since 1981. This fact, that could be seen as producing a positive effect on the future energy scenario, has in fact harmful consequences. As the IEA indicates International Energy Agency (2009), energy investment shows a decadent tendency during the last years, thus slowing the development of new efficient resources and technologies. This decrease is even more patent in renewable power generation, which is expected by the IEA to drop to 20%. Thus, the financial and economic crisis is threatening the achievement of medium term goals in energy consumption and emissions reduction.

Regardless this temporary situation, predictions indicate (International Energy Agency (2009)) that energy demand to be growing again in the Reference Scenario, reaching in 2030 a 40% higher than in 2007, assuming no changes in direction of the present policies. This increase is mainly due to non-OECD countries, in particular China and India, which will show a 53% raise in their energy consumption from 2007 to 2030.

1.1 Energy efficiency in buildings

All this situation motivates the need for focus on the energy efficiency, a concept with increasing significance and that is playing an important role in current energy-saving scenario since encompass energy saving but keeping (or rising) levels of service, productivity, comfort, etc (depending on scope). Some definitions of energy efficiency in buildings can be found in *Directive 2002/91/EC of the European Parliament and of the Council of 16 December 2002 on the*

*Corresponding author: Antonio J. Caamano

energy performance of buildings (n.d.), *Directive 2010/31/EU of the European Parliament and of the Council of 19 May 2010 on the energy performance of buildings (recast)* (n.d.), *Real Decreto 47/2007, de 19 de enero, por el que se aprueba el Procedimiento básico para la certificación de eficiencia energética de edificios de nueva construcción* (n.d.) and Pérez Lombard et al. (2009), but all these can be summarized in: *consuming less energy while providing equal or improved building services.*

As it is apparent from many independent studies ('UNEP (2007), *Directive 2010/31/EU of the European Parliament and of the Council of 19 May 2010 on the energy performance of buildings (recast)* (n.d.) and Pérez Lombard et al. (2009)) the building sector is a key sector for sustainable development and is responsible of almost 40% of total energy consumption. Buildings include a huge set of variables related to energy consumption. Construction materials, HVAC systems, geographical location and orientation, and even use, maintenance and operation are important issues to be taken into account to reach important energy savings and emissions reductions. A great range of policies can be developed associated with any individual variable or the complete set taken as a whole.

One of these policies is the *Directive 2010/31/EU of the European Parliament and of the Council of 19 May 2010 on the energy performance of buildings (recast)* (n.d.), which aims to promote the energy efficiency in buildings. To implement this directive, an energy certification of buildings must be performed. However, at present there is no common or standardized procedure to come up with this certification. The EPBD states the foundation of the energy certification of new and existing buildings through a common methodology to be implemented by every Member State. Calculation must be performed in new buildings and in existing buildings that are subject to major renovation. These buildings must be energy certified to asses their performance in terms of their efficiency. In addition, the EPBD states the need to implement regular inspections of boilers and air-conditioning systems in buildings.

A theoretical research of Meyers et al. (2010), mainly based on Residential Energy Consumption Survey (RECS) from US Department of Energy (US Department of Energy (2001) and US Department of Energy (2005)) and applied to homes, shows that a great deal of energy is wasted in delivering services inefficiently to residents such as heating or cooling unoccupied spaces, overheating/undercooling for whole-house comfort, leakage current, and inefficient appliances. The result of their initial estimate is that over 39% of residential primary energy is wasted.

So, the economic cost of these in situ measurements may be high but it will be offset by a needed reduction of consumption of non-renewable sources of energy.

1.2 WSN and energy efficiency in buildings

Considering the importance of continuous monitoring of power energy parameters of buildings, WSN arise as a feasible solution to reach this continuous monitoring in order to evaluate inefficient energy consumption. However, the nature of the events that lead to energy inefficiency results, impacts on the scalability and performance of operation of the WSN. Taking this limitations into account, it is needed a proposal of a framework for the design and operation of a dense Wireless Sensor Network to detect the inefficient energy consumption in buildings and to gather enough data to improve current procedures to evaluate energy efficiency in buildings. This proposal can be more or less detailed depending on the accuracy level but it has to take into account aspects as important as topology, reliable communication, processing and algorithms of decision.

Jiang et al. (2009a) and Jiang et al. (2009b), WSN are used in order to analyze energy consumption in buildings. This is another approach very different from software engines for energy certification. In both works authors center attention on how to measure AC power consumption using a WSN and how to analyze all gathered measurements. Jiang et al. (2009b) describe the design, deployment, and experience with a Wireless Sensor Network for high-fidelity monitoring of electrical usage in buildings. A network of 38 mote-class AC meters, 6 light sensors, and 1 vibration sensor is used to determine and audit the energy envelope of an active laboratory.

Meyers et al. (2010) do take into account energy use in unoccupied/occupied spaces showing that about 20% of energy is wasted . On the other hand, they consider that wireless sensors are ideal in monitoring as they are easier to install, maintain and replace than wired sensors. Besides, newer sensor technology is capable of performing its own processing without need for a central decision-making hub, opening up possibilities for ad hoc networks for self-organization and control home systems.

de la Campa et al. (2011) propose a scalable framework for distributed detection of energetically inefficient events in buildings using a wireless sensor network. They use the detection of presence in spaces where those events are registered to accurately characterize the energy efficiency of any given building. The theoretical foundations of that work are the basis of the architecture presented here

1.3 Motivation of this work

The need for a common measurement and certification tool for the energy efficiency of buildings is apparent. The measurement tool should be flexible, easy to deploy and maintain and it should require little or no previous adaptation to the specific building being measured. Clearly WSNs are specially well suited for this purpose. However, the capability of such network to operate with little or no supervision is hampered by scalability issues, i.e. the huge number of measurement points to cover the relevant variables throughout the building can compromise the integrity of the data being transmitted. So careful design of the architecture of the wireless sensor network is needed in order to suit the need for reliable sensing, communication, processing, storage and visualization of the parameters that allow the evaluation of the energy efficiency of a building. In this work we present the *NRG-WiSe Building* (Network Reliant GIS, Wireless Sensor Building) architecture, a purpose-built system for effective retrieval, processing and visualization of measurements of energy consumption-related parameters in a building.

This architecture is built to be scalable (its performance is not to be hampered by the number of sensor or gateway nodes)Not only we present the architecture but an effective implementation using commercial off-the-shelf equipment (wireless nodes and gateway-boards). However, the *NRG-WiSe Building* architecture is not limited to the use of such commercial equipment. It is a universal architecture and it can be used with a variety of already available hardware.

1.4 Structure of this work

In Section 2 we overview the general structure of the *NRG-WiSe Building* architecture, presenting the different modules and interfaces connecting them. In Section 3 we present the Sensing Module responsible of the interaction of the sensor and gateway nodes, along with Interfaces I1 (routing protocol) and I2 (interaction of the sensing module with the management module). In Section 4 we proceed to explain the Management Module which allows the (either periodic or event-driven) retrieval of sensed data as well as control of the sensor nodes. Interfaces I2 (description of the interaction with the sensor nodes), I3 (inter-gateway communications), I4 (management decisions), I5 (reception of order from the visualization module) and I6 (transmission of orders to the visualization module) as well as the interaction between interfaces are presented. In Section 5 we present the Visualization Module, responsible for the representation of retrieved data and interaction with the user. Interface I6 (periodic communication with the management module) is presented. Finally, in Section 6 we present the Conclusions and further work to be done.

2. System architecture

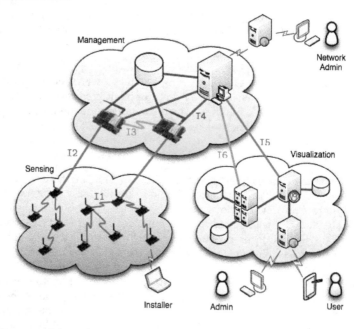

Fig. 1. Architecture of the WSN system for Energy Efficiency measurement in Buildings.

The system comprises three distinct modules: sensing, management and visualisation. In Figure 1 it is shown a general outline of the entire system. Devices that are observed are the three modules and the connections between them. These connections are represented by broken lines in the case of a wireless communication by straight if it is a communication via wired connection. Adjacent to each connection is the name given to the interface between two devices, such as all communications between devices that are used sensing module interface I1. In subsequent sections the three modules are explained in detail, along with the devices and interfaces in the system that make them up.

3. Sensing module

This module is responsible for collecting the data provided by sensors and transmitted to the next module, the management. The measured variables are:

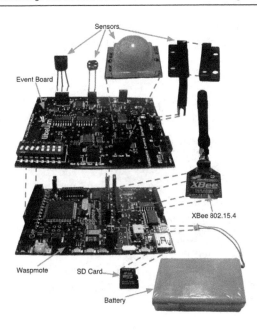

Fig. 2. Connection between sensors and communication module to sensor node.

- **Temperature**. It uses an analog sensor provides a voltage proportional to the measured temperature. The relationship between temperature and output voltage is linear.
- **Brightness**. In this case, choose a resistive sensor whose conductivity varies linearly as a function of the intensity of light received.
- **Presence**. The aim is to detect the presence of people within the facility. We choose a PIR sensor (*Passive Infra-Red*) working in the spectrum of heat radiation of mammals.
- **Open/close passages**. It uses a Hall effect sensor to detect the opening of doors and windows of the facility. This parameter, along with former, it is especially important for the safety of the building, since it allows to detect unauthorized intrusions.

These sensors are integrated into the system through the "Event Board" which provides the company **Libelium** Libelium (n.d.b). This board allows simultaneous connection of multiple sensors of different types. Because you can connect up to eight sensors on the board and that this project uses only four in the future may increase the rate monitored variables. The board connects to the events "Waspmote" manufactured by **Libelium**. This device consists of an ATmega1281 microcontroller and enables the connection of different communication modules. In this project we use the module 802.15.4 XBee-company **Digi**. In Figure 2 it is shown the device used to sense with all its components: sensors, events board, communication module, XBee 802.15.4, battery, SD card and Waspmote device Libelium (n.d.a). Through the red dotted lines represent the connections are between the different elements. The complete system consists of multiple Waspmote with the same structure as that shown in Figure 2. All values measured at each Waspmote must reach the management module and to this end, we define the communications interface I1 between the different devices that make up this module. This interface has all the necessary messages to the routing protocol used, also defined during the development of this project.

3.1 I1 interface. Routing protocol

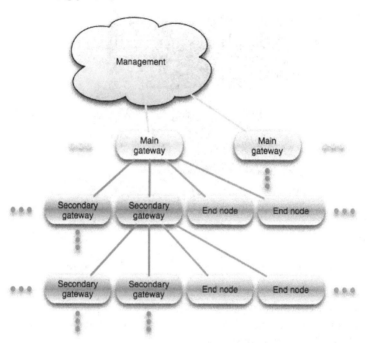

Fig. 3. Hierarchical scheme of the routing protocol.

The interface I1 is used by Waspmote to communicate between them. This interface is used by the routing protocol used in this system and its main feature is that it is hierarchical. It defines three roles a Waspmote can take:

- **Main gateway**. Devices that fulfill this role are at the top of the hierarchy and have direct communication with the management module.
- **Secondary gateway**. In this case, the devices are gateways for other devices of equal or lower rank, but do not have a direct connection with the management module. To carry out its functionality needs to connect to another gateway, either principal or secondary. Ultimately, at least one secondary gateway must be connected to a main.
- **End node**. Devices are the lowest in the hierarchy. For its operation you need a network with a gateway.

In Figure 3 you can see an outline of the hierarchy are devices with different roles in this module. Thereafter, the devices that connect to a gateway will be called "children" and gateways that accept the connection is known as "parents" of such children, following the nomenclature used in object-oriented programming. A secondary runway is both father (with respect to Waspmote that connect to it) and son (with respect to the gateway that connects with itself). Because Waspmote have a memory limitation, fix the maximum number children each gateway can have eight of each type, ie type eight children and eight children secondary runway type end node. However, eight children are secondary gateways can in turn have children of both types, making this fact does not imply any limitation for the entire system.

The interface messages have I1 are:

- IMALIVE. Message sent by broadcast periodically by all devices, regardless of the role they have. In Figure 4 represents the structure of this type of message. The field Type uniquely identifies the package and the P represents the priority of this package, these two fields common to all packages. The *flag* G indicates whether the Waspmote in question is an end node (G = 0) or a gateway (G = 1). To differentiate between the two types of gateways using the *flag* A that indicates whether the main gateway (A = 1) or secondary (A = 0). The *flag* R is used to indicate whether a device is searching for parent process (R = 1) or if it has completed this process, it is not necessary to be the Waspmote a main walkway (R = 0). Finally, the *flag* F is enabled (F = 1) indicates that a gateway can receive messages of type FLUSH.

Fig. 4. Message Type IMALIVE.

- GWREPLY. Message generated by a gateway that receives a message IMALIVE with the *flag* R = 1. He is sent by *unicast* to the device that caused the generation of this message. In Figure 5 can observe the structure of this type of package.

Fig. 5. Message Type GWREPLY.

- GWACK. Waspmote message sent by a father looking after having received at least one message of type GWREPLY. It is used to inform a specific gateway that from receipt of this message has a new son. The structure of this message is represented in Figure 6.

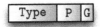

Fig. 6. Message Type GWACK.

- GWASSIGN. This type of message is used to change the role of an end-node device is a secondary gateway. He is sent by *Waspmote unicast* to the role that will change. In Figure 7 represents the structure of these messages.
- GWACCEPT. Message sent in response to confirm receipt of a GWASSIGN and its structure is depicted in Figure 8.

Fig. 7. Message Type GWASSIGN.

Fig. 8. Message Type GWACCEPT.

- BUNDLEREQ. This type of message is used to explicitly request any data Waspmote sensors. Its structure is shown in Figure 9. The field NMV is used to indicate the number of fields VIA MAC that follow. For its part, the fields VIA MAC are the way you have to keep this package to reach the device recipient of this message. This recipient is not included in the fields VIA MAC, but his ID is in the SENS MAC. Both the VIA MAC as SENS MAC is a unique identifier in the system Waspmote and are formed by the last three bytes of the MAC address of the communications module 802.15.4 XBee-each device. If a Waspmote receives this message and have to resend it takes care of removing the identifier VIA MAC upgrade package and the NMV.

Fig. 9. Message Type BUNDLEREQ.

- BUNDLEREP. Main message of the system responsible for transmitting to the management system data collected from the sensors. In Figure 10 shows the scheme of this type of message. As for the fields has not yet explained, the PL indicates the number of bytes transmitted in this packet, including header. The *flags* indicated in capital letters refer to the last device that have gone through, while the *flags* indicated in lowercase letters refer to the device that generated this message. The six fields TS are the time stamp when the measurements have been traveling on this package. Fields TV [i] are only indicative of the type of sensor that has been measured, the value appears in the V [i] follows. For this message, each gateway that receives and forwards it adds a new field VIA MAC and updates the field NMV.

- FLUSH. A message containing one or more messages of type BUNDLEREP complete. Through these messages, a gateway that has had a temporary problem to her father is sending the messages Bundlerep has been stored on the SD card available to Waspmote. In Figure 11 represents the structure of this type of message. The field nb indicating the number of messages BUNDLEREP complete that are transmitted in this packet.

Type	P	PL		NMV	G	g	a	RESERVED
TS		TS			TS			
TS		TS			TS			
MAC VIA [1]								
...								
MAC VIA [n]								
MAC SENS								
TV[1]		V[1]			TV[2]			
...		V[n]			TV[n]			

Fig. 10. Message Type BUNDLEREP.

Type	P	NB	BUNDLEREP[1]
		...	
BUNDLEREP[n]			

Fig. 11. Message Type FLUSH.

- GWDELETE. Message sent by a gateway when it receives a message type BUNDLEREP a device that is not his child. When a device receives this message (represented in Figure 12), restart the process of finding a father.

Fig. 12. Message Type GWDELETE.

Once known the structure of all the messages used, it is necessary to comment that they do not have the same priority when being sent and the time to be served by the Waspmote that it has received. Table 1 indicates the priority of each message, taking into account the priority 0 is the highest and the 3 is the lowest.

Table 1. Message priority in Interface I1.

0	1	2	3
GWASSIGN	GWACK	IMALIVE	FLUSH
	GWACCEPT	GWREPLY	
	BUNDLEREQ	BUNDLEREP	
	GWDELETE		

3.2 Interface I2. Management module communication

As in the previous case, for the use of the interface I2, we have defined a communication protocol. In Figure 1 shows that only certain Waspmote have communication with the management module. These Waspmote fulfill the role of main walkway and connected via the serial port of the aforementioned devices module. The messages are available for this interface are:

- WGWASSIGN. This message has the same functionality as the message GWASSIGN THE INTERFACE I1, ie, changing the role of Waspmote recipient. In this case the device becomes the main gateway. Its structure is identical to the message of type GWASSIGN and can be seen in Figure 13.

Fig. 13. Message Type WGWASSIGN.

- WGWACCEPT. In this case, as in the previous one, this type of message has the same functionality as the namesake of his in the interface I1, but its structure (see Figure 14) changes slightly. The two new fields are the last two bytes of the address own MAC and used to create unique identifiers in the management module.

Fig. 14. Message Type WGWACCEPT.

- WBUNDLEREQ. This message has the same functionality and the message structure of type BUNDLEREQ. When a Waspmote receive such messages and is not directed to itself simply forwarded by the interface I1. The message structure is shown in Figure 15.

Type	P	NMV
MAC VIA [1]		
...		
MAC VIA [n]		
MAC SENS		

Fig. 15. Message Type WBUNDLEREQ.

- WBUNDLEREP. Again, it has the same functionality and structure (see Figure 16) that the message of type BUNDLEREP. In this case the primary gateway is simple bridge between the interface interface I1 and I2.
- WFLUSH. The representation of this type of message is done in Figure 17 and we can see that is almost identical to the structure of the messages FLUSH. This difference is due to the standardization of nomenclature, since the messages BUNDLEREP and WBUNDLEREP are identical. Also identical are the messages FLUSH and WFLUSH.

Following the similarities with the interface I1, the messages presented in the above lines do not have the same priority when being sent to the management system or the time to be served by the Waspmote. It should be mentioned that the interface messages I2 share priority structures with interface messages I1. Therefore, if a message is processed with

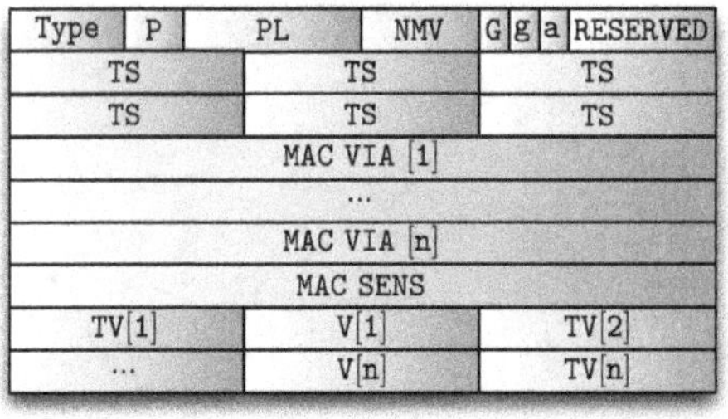

Type	P	PL	NMV	G	g	a	RESERVED
TS		TS		TS			
TS		TS		TS			
MAC VIA [1]							
...							
MAC VIA [n]							
MAC SENS							
TV[1]		V[1]		TV[2]			
...		V[n]		TV[n]			

Fig. 16. Message Type WBUNDLEREP.

Type	P	NB	WBUNDLEREP[1]
			...
WBUNDLEREP[n]			

Fig. 17. Message Type WFLUSH.

higher priority, regardless of the interface to which it belongs . Table 2 indicates the priority of each message.

0	1	2	3
WGWASSIGN	WBUNDLEREQ	WBUNDLEREP	WFLUSH
WGWACCEPT			

Table 2. Message priority in Interface I2.

3.3 Interaction between interfaces

In order to improve understanding of the logic are the devices that make this module, flow charts represent the following three types of Waspmote in Figures 18, 19 and 20. Specifically, the first of them represents a flow diagram which fulfils the role Waspmote end node in the second case shows the role of the secondary runway and, finally, the third represents the case of main gateway role. For a better understanding is necessary to explain the symbology of flowsheets represented. First, the rectangles represent different actions. There are two colors, yellow identifies the actions related to the interface I1, while blue is used for actions related to the interface I2. The circles are used to indicate "points" in the code the program does output to multiple actions. The red hexagon labeled "Stop" means the changing role of the Waspmote other, thus changing the flow chart to follow when possible actions to take. In terms of transitions between actions using arrows. A is attached "Periodic" and use the blue to indicate that the actions are performed periodically.

4. Management module

The management module is the standard software that transforms the raw data from the sensing hardware to software page for the presentation of the display module. Following the View-Controller programming model but applied to a complex system, the management

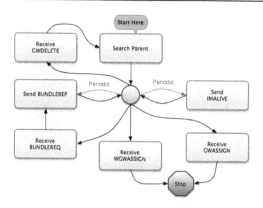

Fig. 18. Flow chart of a node with end node role.

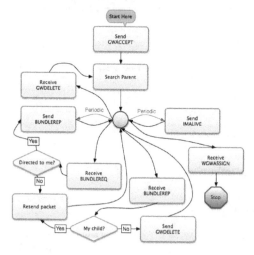

Fig. 19. Flow chart of a node with secondary gateway role.

module itself would be the system controller, which does not exempt himself from having his own data presentation software for the administrator the network.

The management module objectives are:

- Perform monitoring and management of the network intercom ALIX Engines (n.d.) boards together by SNMP.
- Store information collected by the sensor network that connects ALIX to each plate.
- Establish and launch alarms required by the user from the display module.
- Send commands acting on the sensor network.
- To receive, interpret and manage the orders of the display module.
- Submit the information display module to be represented.

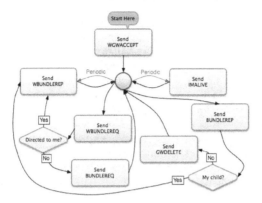

Fig. 20. Flow chart of a node with main gateway role..

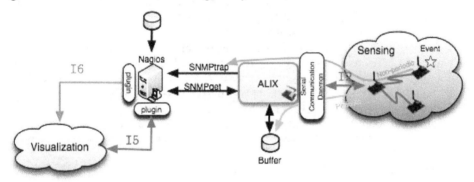

Fig. 21. Management module architecture.

The management module architecture is shown in Figure 21. It consists of the following elements:

- Apache Web server. The web portal is the system chosen for the interaction of the network administrator. For a network administrator, the management server already contains everything you need to detect network problems before they occur or have occurred, and perform preventive maintenance and corrective. For this reason, information from the network management server does not need to be integrated into the display module, which is oriented to the visualization of data sensing. Since the interaction between network administrator and server management is done from a web interface, Apache is the foundation of the web portal administration.

- Nagios Server network management. Mounted on the Nagios Nagios (n.d.) server Apache allows to separate the management of the backbone that supports the sensor network for managing sensing information, enabling you to plan upgrades and maintenance of the network in advance, so affecting as little as possible to services it provides. In a broad sense, it can be considered to the display module as a plugin to integrate monitoring and management of buildings in Nagios, but the separation is so great, that formally it is not. Management information is viewed by network specialist with disabilities who display the information on what is happening in a building, while the process of acquiring information and responding to alerts is similar. That is why Nagios is used not only for network management, but also to make the process of data acquisition and control alerts. To understand this better, we could say that you could use Nagios to represent the information associated with the operation of the sensing hardware, what settings have IEEE802.15.4 IEEE (n.d.b) Digi radios, or what speed is set the serial port between ALIX and Waspmote. The professional who will go to the website for this information will keep in mind that should foresee bottlenecks in the network, or interference associated with the use of certain frequencies in wireless transmission, but when it comes to room temperature, measured with the hardware , the network administrator who can not say how they are performing heat transfer between rooms or how to interpret the values ??present in each room.

Apart from monitoring the technical components that make up the system from the point of view of the protocols, servers, applications and network infrastructure, Nagios is also responsible for alerting the values ??stored in their databases, which includes alerts the values ??measured by the sensing module.

- Nagios Plugins intercom with display module. In this system, two plugins are built on Nagios. The mission of these plugins is interfacing with the display module and, in fact, each plugin corresponds to a system interface (I5 and I6). The plugin for receipt of orders of the display module, which implements the interface I5, takes place, controlled by XML-RPC Foundation (n.d.a) requests:

  - Communication with OpenLayers Openlayers (n.d.) and Open Flash Chart Chart (n.d.), receiving such requests for information and translating them to messages snmpget.
  - The establishment of internal alerts in Nagios.
  - The message generation snmpset to the ALIX boards, in order to translate these messages into the sensor network.

  The plugin for communication of information to the display module, which implements the interface I6, sends them through XML-RPC response, the requested data to Nagios to represent the maps and graphs that allow the display of information sensing .

- ALIX Serial Port communication daemon. This daemon, which runs on the operating system boards ALIX (voyage distribution of GNU/Linux for embedded systems) Voyage (n.d.). It performs three functions which are essential for communication between the management module and the sensing module:

  - it manages and operates the serial port on the ALIX boards, to enable communication between ALIX and Waspmote gateway.
  - it interprets the commands received from the sensor network, translating them into SNMP messages.
  - it interprets the messages received from the server SNMP management protocol messages translating a network of sensors.

- Daemon SNMPTRAP message reception. In the management server, resides a demon in charge of listening to any type messages generated from SNMPTRAP ALIX boards. The meaning of these messages is that the sensor network and the plates themselves ALIX can send urgent messages or associated with events that can not wait to be consulted by snmpget.

- Database MySQL sensing buffering. In order to distribute the management traffic properly and that its intensity can be controlled from the management server with all the information from non-urgent ALIX boards is stored in an intermediate database that acts as a buffer, waiting for snmpget message management server can be answered with this information, and deleted from the database.

- Private MIB (Management Information Base) sensing. The introduction of the sensor network as an element to manage, requires the creation of a private MIB IETF (n.d.a), which implements the new items you want to monitor or manage. Because you can not enter directly managing sensor motes, since it would oblige them to implement SNMP protocol (and there are devices with processing power and limited storage), their management is done indirectly directed by ALIX boards. Thus, the sensing information MIB is implemented in ALIX boards, and is known by the management server. When you need to retrieve information in a sensor network, the management server asks for your object in the MIB to the ALIX board, and this is a gateway to the sensor network, and translate that request to the protocol of the sensor network if it does not already have the required information in its buffer.

4.1 Interface I2. Sensing module communications

For communication with the sensing module, the management module interface uses I2. This interface is implemented from the management side of the module by a demon living in the ALIX board, which is the communication daemon ALIX serial port, as explained in the previous section.

4.2 Interface I3. Inter-gateway communications

Communication between ALIX boards is performed using the system interconnection model TCP / IP, and involves essentially the following protocols:

- IEEE802.11a IEEE (n.d.a), to the extent of quality of service (QoS footnote Quality of Service) 802.11e IEEE (n.d.a). This is the network layer protocol stack and is responsible for carrying information between 2 machines. IEEE802.11a is a wireless communication protocol and uses OFDM modulation to provide bit rates of 54Mbps at the physical level, which often result in at rates up to 28Mbps IP with optimal transmission conditions. The working frequency band of 5GHz is, and therefore generally exempt from most of the interference from other devices inside a building (which used to be located in the 2.4 GHz).

- IP. For communication between ALIX, and the rest of the system, Internet Protocol Version 4 is in use, because it is the most widespread protocol interred in virtually all types of computer networks worldwide.

- OLSR (Optimized Link State Routing). For the auto-routing between ALIX boards used OLSR IETF (n.d.b) with ETX metric to look at the specifics of routing over wireless networks, where sometimes a greater number of network hops does not imply a worse way, if the conditions of the links are better than the path of least number of hops between.

4.3 Interface I4. Management decisions

Communication between ALIX and the management server is based on the same protocols as the interface I3, but with the addition of also using network management protocol SNMP

(Simple Network Management Protocol). To query SNMP MIB need to exist to define the objects that has to ask, and similarly, there needs to exist side management agents managed elements to implement the form in which has to recover the value of each object queried. For ALIX boards, the standard MIB information on the various components of the system and the network between ALIX (CPU load, available memory, signal level on the links, etc), add the definition a MIB own recovery sensing information. This MIB resides in the ALIX boards and the management server, and is implemented by ALIX boards.

Specifically, SNMP messages used in the inter-ALIX - Nagios are:

- snmpget - Used to retrieve the newspaper sensing data have been properly stored temporarily in a MySQL MySQL (n.d.) database on ALIX boards.
- SNMPresponse - The ALIX boards used to return the values ??requested by the management server.
- snmpset - are sent from the management server ALIX boards, and serve both to alter values ??set in the various elements managed ALIX boards, to implement actuators of the sensor network. Can also be used to set up alerts monitored by sensors.
- SNMPTRAP - SNMP messages are sent from ALIX boards to inform, without prior request from the management server, urgent information associated with events. Usually used for transmitting high priority messages and sensors whose values ??are not important, but the events that arise from the transition of its states. For example, in the case of Hall effect sensors, it makes more sense to report on the opening or closing a window or door, to report periodically to the window or door is open or closed. Server-side management, a demon is responsible for hearing such messages and integrate the information received it with the rest of the information management platform.

4.4 Interface I5. Reception of orders from visualization module

In the management server there is a plugin developed to meet the receive orders from the display module, usually expressly ordered by end-users of the system. Communication between management and display modules is performed using the protocol for remote procedure call XML-RPC. Specifically, the interface I5, queries involving XML-RPC that are made from the display module. However, this plugin is detailed further in the next section.

4.5 Interface I6. Sending information towards visualization module

To respond to XML-RPC queries made?by the display module, also implemented a Nagios plugin that performs the necessary tasks in the interface I6. The main task is to gather the information management server to respond to XML-RPC queries to generate the answers to those queries, and send them to the parts of the display module that required information through the interface I5 . In the next section provides more detail of this Nagios plugin.

4.6 Interaction between interfaces

In Figure 22 it is shown the message exchange that occurs in the management module when there are periodic measurements.

We can summarize the sequence as follows:

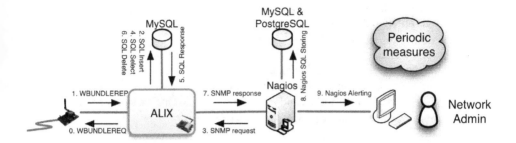

Fig. 22. Message chain in a periodic sensing process.

1. (optional). WBundleReq. If the user explicitly requested a soda from the sensing information from the display module, it generates a message requesting information. If not, just wait for the periodic sending of the sensors.
2. WBundleRep. Comes from the message Waspmote measuring sensors.
3. is inserted into the MySQL DB that serves as an intermediate buffer between the sensor network management server and Nagios. Remain there until the server ask for that information management.
4. The management server periodically collects information via snmpget requests.
5. The management agent ALIX board, upon receiving a request snmpget, look at the private MIB of sensors, and notes that to retrieve the requested information, you have to access the database sensing buffering, so making the query to the database.
6. The DB responds with the requested data.
7. Since the data will be sent to Nagios, are deleted from the DB of ALIX.
8. The management agent responds to snmpget with information from the DB in an SNMP response.
9. Nagios stores the information received at its own DB.
10. (optional). If any of the values ??exceeds some threshold, the administrator is alerted.

In Figure 23 it is shown the message exchange that occurs when an event occurs in the sensor network.

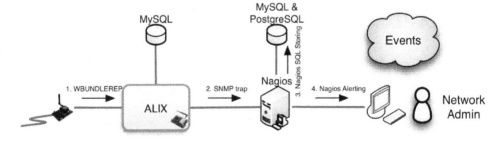

Fig. 23. Message exchange that occurs when an event occurs in the sensor network.

The sequence is as follows:

1. An event occurs (for example, a door is opened), and this translates to a message that reaches WBundleRep ALIX board.
2. The communication daemon ALIX serial port recognizes the message as an event that must be transmitted immediately and not stored in the intermediate buffer, so it generates a message to the server SNMPTRAP Nagios.
3. The snmptrapd daemon, which manages the reception of SNMPTRAP messages on UDP port 162, it receives the trap and resends it to Nagios, which makes storage in its own DB.
4. If applicable, it generates an alert to the administrator.

5. Visualization module

The Visualization module has two main objectives:

- Provide information to the user.
- Manage the interaction system ↔ user.

To complement this functionality, the module must retrieve information from the sensing module, processed by the management module, and provide additional processing to provide the user with useful information. Therefore, sensing and communication between users is not done directly but always through the management module.

The display module architecture is detailed in Figure 24.

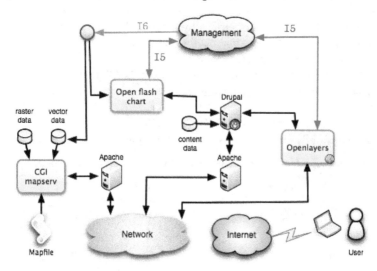

Fig. 24. Visualization Module Architecture.

For the presentation of information, given that the scenario is the energy efficiency in buildings, uses two visualization schemes:

- A map-based display vector layers navigable semitransparent overlays. Thus, the user has real time and at a single glance, general information on all variables measured in the building shown on the same plane (Figure 25).

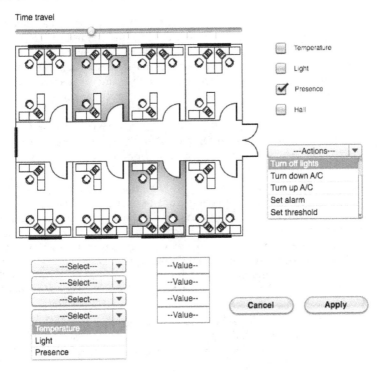

Fig. 25. User interaction over a vector floor plan.

- A graphics-based visualization. With this display you can analyze historical sensor on each node, making comparisons between various graphics, easily detecting events in the securities, as well as the establishment of specific alerts when values ??are generated above or below certain thresholds (Figure 26).

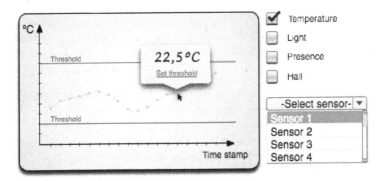

Fig. 26. User interaction over a graphics view.

To function, the display module makes use of:

- Apache Web Servers Apache (n.d.). The web information is presented as this is the route that offers more independence from the user terminal and the rest of the system. It has a web server as a gateway to the system of maps WFS (Web Feature Server) and WMS (Web Map Server) defined by the OGC (Open Geospatial Consortium) OpenGIS (n.d.), as well as other web server (which may optionally be the same) that serves the interaction interface with the user. It is therefore of the first layer, which manages software involved in the system (HTTP communication).

- Drupal CMS (Content Management System) . On the Apache server that serves the graphical interface, install the Drupal Drupal (n.d.) CMS, which facilitates the creation of the interface. Due to its size and broad support from the community of free software, allows in the future to extend its functionality.

  The content management system brings to the construction of the web portal of information around what is not displaying maps or charts. Manages issues of different nature and importance of graphic design ranging from the portal (font, structure, headers and footers, links, etc.) to manage access rights to information (roles), authentication, connection to databases, and so on. By way of analogy, we might say that while Apache would be the foundation and the building facade, Drupal is the circuitry, the air conditioning system, alarm, lighting, plumbing and everything that makes a building can provide generic services without going into detail on what type of service provided by the building.

- Mapserver map server. Using Apache to support geographic information subsystem, is constituted as Mapserver Foundation (n.d.b) WMS and WFS, distributing the graphical interface maps and plans on which information is represented. Figure 27 shows the internal architecture of Mapserver.

  Mapserver as WMS and WFS uses the information stored as raster and vector data to compose a final image that maps customer service. Raster data are satellite maps and aerial photos free, which serve as base layer above them, capture dynamic information graphically. Vector data are an ordered set of points, lines and polygons that occur in layers on raster images. Thus, from an appropriate zoom level map on a building, it will overlap the layer that represents the plane of the top floor of the building, with the option to enable or disable semitransparent layers that represent information associated with this floor. For example, if you want to graphically represent the temperature in the rooms on the top floor of a building, a raster layer is a layer superimposed lines and polygons representing the plane of the floor of the building, and on this, be presented another layer of semitransparent polygons whose color will vary depending on temperature values ??being measured in each room instantly. When the user increases the zoom sufficiently, the layers that represent the information on the top floor disappear and appear to represent the penultimate floor, and so on up through all the floors.

- Client Openlayers maps. Integrated as a module in Drupal, for viewing the maps, mapping the client uses WMC (Web Map Client) Openlayers, which generally consists of a JavaScript library that facilitates the integration of maps and layers loaded from different sources into a web page.

  In the display of maps of the information could be used only Mapserver, but to integrate the functionality of Mapserver on a website that offers many more services than the representation of maps using OpenLayers. Openlayers provides maps in addition to the navigability and the layer of user interaction. For example, is responsible for the Time Travel " tool"that occurs in the software. This tool enables " time travel"back

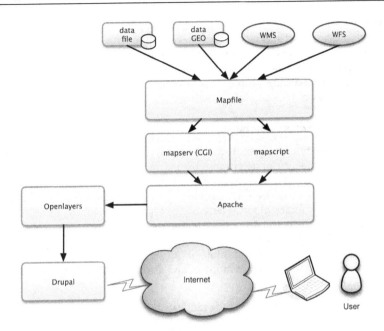

Fig. 27. Mapserver's internal architecture.

on the map representing the graphical information not only of what is sensing in real time in the building, but to represent the state of the building at any moment ago he was being sensed. The management module is stored all this information, and therefore Openlayers is responsible for providing the user with an interface as simple as a scroll bar, which, however, translated into the appropriate messages between the management module and the display to to recover the information associated with a particular time of historic building and is represented in vector layers superimposed on the map Mapserver. Openlayers is also responsible for the " Filters"tool on the maps, which allows the application to graphical information represented filters that make it more specific, such as vector layers represent colors that show only the temperature of those rooms on not detected the presence and the luminosity exceeds a certain threshold (to detect, for example, lights on unnecessarily). By managing the translation of user gestures to messages in the system, Openlayers also be responsible for the shutdown command of these lights on in vain.

- Open Flash Chart Interactive Graphics. Charts configured within Drupal module allows the user to interact with the graphics, view historical comparisons and identify alarms in the system.

To view system information using a different paradigm different from the representation of data, the system supports graphical visualization thanks to Open Flash Chart. Its functionality is equivalent to Openlayers, in the sense that it allows actions like this, but to present information differently, the system adapts better to the type of user. While there is more intuitive actions performed on a map of the building, such as monitoring the condition of the building, others may find it easier to see them on graphs. For example, the equivalent of " Tool Time"in the travel map display is the X axis of the graphs, since the values ??are plotted versus time, and this makes while with " Time Travel "is easy to see global temperature transitions of a building and the heat flows that occur throughout the day on a graph is easily detected high, low, medium and value comparisons. Open Flash Chart is communicated through the same API that the plugin Openlayers management server that receives orders visualization software.

5.1 Interface I5. User-sensor interaction

Interface I5 is responsible for generating the corresponding messages in the management modules and sensing when a user determines the performance of an action or instant retrieval of information. It is one of the two interfaces that connect the management module to the display module and involves a management plugin Nagios server, which receives the user's request, and the library OpenLayers, or the Open Flash Chart software on the side display module, who are mandated generate the user's request. When a user interacts with a map served by Openlayers, and this interaction requires retrieval of information or sending message to the management module or the sensing module automatically generates the request to the plugin management module, and also occurs when the interaction is via a graphical served by Open Flash Chart.

You may order several actions by any of the modes:

- Instant retrieval of data. It results in an application to the management module to a snmpget ALIX boards and recovery of the last values measured for each sensor. This is a direct interaction between user and management module, as in response to user action, several messages are exchanged between the display and management modules. In practice it is a refresh button to display the images used to test at a time when network problems arise. If the soda works, it means that the whole chain of intermediate software layer protocols and are doing their jobs. Additionally, it also gives the user knowledge about the latency of the entire system.

- Performance. The elements are controlled by actuators connected to the sensors may be activated or deactivated user's express request. This interaction is direct between user and sensor (or actuator), since in response to user action, a number of messages generated in the display module, management module cross and reach the sensing module. Figure 28 represents the chain of messages that occurs in the system when a user decides to send a message of action.

The sequence would be the following:

1. The user requests an action through the Drupal CMS, using a chart or map for it (or Open Flash Chart Openlayers).
2. Using XML-RPC request, Openlayers or Open Flash Chart requests the plugin that implements the interface I5 acting.
3. Nagios generates a snmpset message with information from the actuator to activate the sensor location of your partner, who travels to the ALIX board, where the sensing MIB translates the command to snmpset ACTION devil sends his port control series to reach the gateway Waspmote is connected.
4. The ACTION message travels across the network of sensors to the actuator, producing the requested action.

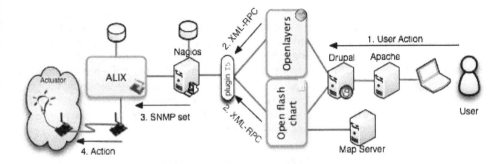

Fig. 28. Chain of messages that occurs in the system when a user send an action message.

There are three modes of operation:

- switching. Based on relays or digital switches, is on or off of the elements on which you want to act. An example might be the ignition of an engine, or the lights without the possibility of graduating the intensity of light. It can be done from the motes sensors used in the project (Waspmote) using plates Libelium distributed by the company for that purpose (Prototyping Boards).

- The analog performance. Granularity based on variable outputs, accurately regulates the voltage delivered to the element on which it acts. An example would be to set the intensity of light from a luminaire with the possibility of graduating the intensity of light emitted. It can be done from the motes

- The performance schedule. For more complex elements such as air conditioning, where there are many variables beyond the set on or off a device, or regulation of the intensity of current or voltage at one point, the system foresees the creation of plugins in the management software to interact with them. Thus, the display module present a common API (Application Programming Interface) action would implement different modules programmed in software management mode drivers for performance against each type of complex.

- Setting Alarms. You may want to measure thresholds are exceeded alarms when higher or lower. Alarms can generate informational messages to the user, or may have associated actions. The alarm information on the user side leave the decision about what action to take, while the performance alarms generate automatic messages to the sensing module and activate / deactivate an actuator without further user intervention.

Alarms can be set at two different levels:

- managed by the sensor alarms. These alarms have only the information of the sensor, and are generated by it. Its use reduces the network load when not needed more information than can provide a sensor itself, distributing the processing load of the alarms. As an example, imagine a Hall effect sensor on a door. Because all the information about the opening of the door is contained in the sensor itself does not make sense to generate unnecessary messages between modules. Additionally, because the door opening is a discrete event (the door goes from open to closed state or vice versa) does not make sense to report the status of the door or window, but rather the transition, and therefore the self-reporting state transition is itself an event alarm.

– alarms managed by the management module. These alarms can rely on the information from all sensors. They sense when it is necessary to obtain more than one sensor to generate an alarm. For example, we could determine that because of the location of various sensors in a room temperature results in different measurements, despite being the same room, since the temperature is not uniform throughout the room. However, because the air conditioning system is unique in acting on the system must take into account all measurements (either by establishing an average, weighted differently each measure, etc). In this situation, the alarm must be established by the management module, which knows all sensor measurements.

5.2 Interface I6. Periodic communication with management module

The management module periodically collects information from both ALIX boards and the network between them (SNMPgets) as a sensing module (protocol of the sensor network). This information has to be sent to the user interface, and for this task implements the interface I8, which interconnects the management and display modules.

Just like the interface I5 asynchronously receives user commands from the management and/or sensing modules. The interface I6 synchronously returns the information reported by the sensors whose measurement range is periodic, as well as asynchronous communications for events and alarms, or refresh the user requested information.

The fate of the information from the management software can be one of the following (or both):

• The vector database that generates the map of Mapserver. To display the map according to the configuration required by the user.
• Charts Drupal module. To display a chart with the information required.

Figure 29 shows the message exchange that occurs when a user requests information from management module, and how the interface I6 involved in the process.

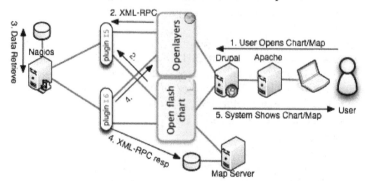

Fig. 29. Message exchange that occurs when a user requests information from management module.

The sequence would be the following:

1. The user opens a chart or map, agreeing with it, through Apache + Drupal, Open Flash Chart or OpenLayers.

2. Open Flash Chart or Openlayers automatically generated XML-RPC request to the plugin I5 of Nagios.
3. Nagios recovers from database data, which then delivered to your plugin I6.
4. Depending on who requested the information, the plugin I6 sends the response XML-RPC or Openlayers Open Flash Char.
5. Drupal via Apache shows the user the chart or map.

6. Conclusions and future work

We have addressed the problem of developing an architecture for Wireless Sensor Networks which are to be efficient and scalable in the purpose of gathering energy efficiency information in buildings. We have presented a complete description of the *NRG-WiSe Building*. Although the problem has been addressed recently by other researchers, to the best of the knowledge of the authors, no complete description of such an architecture has been proposed until the present work. With readily available hardware and software tools we have built a functioning architecture for a wireless sensor network that retrieves and presents energy efficiency events in buildings, allows interaction of the user with both the data and the sensor nodes and which performance is not hurt by the number of nodes in the building.

At present, a first instance of the proposed network with over a hundred sensor nodes, each one purporting four different sensors (temperature, light, presence and passage control), is being deployed in Fuenlabrada Campus of the Rey Juan Carlos University. Extensive testing of such network is to take place in order to experimentally validate the architecture presented here, thus providing an invaluable tool, both accurate and easily deployable, for characterization of the energy efficiency of buildings.

7. Acknowledgements

The authors wish to thank Sergio A. de la Campa, Ana B. Rodríguez-González and Javier Ramos for fruitful discussions that led to the improvement of the present work. This work has been partially supported by Research Grants TEC2009-12098 and TEC2010-19263 from the Ministry of Science and Innovation of the Spanish Government.

8. References

Apache (n.d.). Apache software web page, http://www.apache.org/.
Chart, O. F. (n.d.). Open flash chart software web page, http://openflashchart.com/.
de la Campa, S., RodrÃguez-GonzÃ¡lez, A., Ramos, J. & CaamaÃ±o, A. (2011). Distributed detection of events for evaluation of energy efficiency in buildings, *New Technologies, Mobility and Security (NTMS), 2011 4th IFIP International Conference on*, pp. 1 –6.
Directive 2002/91/EC of the European Parliament and of the Council of 16 December 2002 on the energy performance of buildings (n.d.). *Official Journal of the European Communities* . 4 Jan. 2003, pp. 65–71.
Directive 2010/31/EU of the European Parliament and of the Council of 19 May 2010 on the energy performance of buildings (recast) (n.d.). *Official Journal of the European Communities* . , 18 Jun. 2010, pp. 13–35.
Drupal (n.d.). Drupal software web page, http://drupal.org/.
Engines, P. (n.d.). Alix board product specification page, http://pcengines.ch/alix.htm.

Foundation, A. S. (n.d.a). Apache xml-rpc, http://ws.apache.org/xmlrpc/.

Foundation, O. S. G. (n.d.b). Mapserver software web page, http://mapserver.org/.

IEEE (n.d.a). 802.11a-1999 - ieee standard for telecommunications and information exchange between systems - lan/man specific requirements - part 11: Wireless medium access control (mac) and physical layer (phy) specifications: High speed physical layer in the 5 ghz band, http://standards.ieee.org/findstds/standard/802.11a-1999.html.

IEEE (n.d.b). 802.15.4-2003 ieee standard for telecommunications and information exchange between systems - lan/man specific requierements - part 15: Wireless medium access control (mac) and physical layer (phy) specifications for low rate wireless personal area networks (wpan), http://standards.ieee.org/findstds/standard/802.15.4-2003.html.

IETF (n.d.a). Rfc3418 - management information base (mib) for the simple network management protocol (snmp), http://tools.ietf.org/html/rfc3418.

IETF (n.d.b). Rfc3626 - optimized link state routing protocol (olsr), http://tools.ietf.org/html/rfc3626.

International Energy Agency (2009). World energy outlook: 2009 fact sheet. Why is our current energy pathway unsustainable?, IEA Publications.

Jiang, X., Ly, M. V., Taneja, J., Dutta, P. & Culler, D. (2009a). Design and implementation of a high-fidelity ac metering network, *IPSN09* .

Jiang, X., Ly, M. V., Taneja, J., Dutta, P. & Culler, D. (2009b). Experiences with a high-fidelity wireless building energy auditing network, *SenSys09* .

Libelium (n.d.a). Waspmote product specification page, http://www.libelium.com/products/waspmote.

Libelium (n.d.b). Website, http://www.libelium.com/.

Meyers, R. J., Williams, E. D. & Matthews, H. S. (2010). Scoping the potential of monitoring and control technologies to reduce energy use in homes, *Energy and Buildings* 42(5): 563 – 569.

MySQL (n.d.). Mysql software web page, http://www.mysql.com/.

Nagios (n.d.). Nagios software web page, http://www.nagios.org/.

OpenGIS, O. G. C. (n.d.). Ogc web page, http://www.opengeospatial.org/.

Openlayers (n.d.). Openlayers software web page, http://openlayers.org/.

Pérez Lombard, L., Ortiz, J., González, R. & Maestre, I. R. (2009). A review of benchmarking, rating and labelling concepts within the framework of building energy certification schemes, *Energy and Buildings* 41: 272–278.

Real Decreto 47/2007, de 19 de enero, por el que se aprueba el Procedimiento básico para la certificación de eficiencia energética de edificios de nueva construcción (n.d.). Boletín Oficial del Estado . , 31 Jan. 2007, pp. 4499–4507.

UNEP (2007). *Buildings and climate change: status, challenges and opportunities*, United Nations Environment Programme.

US Department of Energy (2001). Residential Energy Consumption Survey (RECS), Energy Information Administration.
    URL: *http://www.eia.doe.gov/emeu/recs/recs2001/detail_tables.html*

US Department of Energy (2005). Residential Energy Consumption Survey (RECS), Energy Information Administration.
    URL: *http://www.eia.doe.gov/emeu/recs/recs2005/hc2005_tables/detailed_tables2005.html*

Voyage (n.d.). Voyage gnu/linux distribution for embedded systems, http://linux.voyage.hk/.

Permissions

The contributors of this book come from diverse backgrounds, making this book a truly international effort. This book will bring forth new frontiers with its revolutionizing research information and detailed analysis of the nascent developments around the world.

We would like to thank Sameh Gobriel, for lending his expertise to make the book truly unique. He has played a crucial role in the development of this book. Without his invaluable contribution this book wouldn't have been possible. He has made vital efforts to compile up to date information on the varied aspects of this subject to make this book a valuable addition to the collection of many professionals and students.

This book was conceptualized with the vision of imparting up-to-date information and advanced data in this field. To ensure the same, a matchless editorial board was set up. Every individual on the board went through rigorous rounds of assessment to prove their worth. After which they invested a large part of their time researching and compiling the most relevant data for our readers. Conferences and sessions were held from time to time between the editorial board and the contributing authors to present the data in the most comprehensible form. The editorial team has worked tirelessly to provide valuable and valid information to help people across the globe.

Every chapter published in this book has been scrutinized by our experts. Their significance has been extensively debated. The topics covered herein carry significant findings which will fuel the growth of the discipline. They may even be implemented as practical applications or may be referred to as a beginning point for another development. Chapters in this book were first published by InTech; hereby published with permission under the Creative Commons Attribution License or equivalent.

The editorial board has been involved in producing this book since its inception. They have spent rigorous hours researching and exploring the diverse topics which have resulted in the successful publishing of this book. They have passed on their knowledge of decades through this book. To expedite this challenging task, the publisher supported the team at every step. A small team of assistant editors was also appointed to further simplify the editing procedure and attain best results for the readers.

Our editorial team has been hand-picked from every corner of the world. Their multi-ethnicity adds dynamic inputs to the discussions which result in innovative outcomes. These outcomes are then further discussed with the researchers and contributors who give their valuable feedback and opinion regarding the same. The feedback is then collaborated with the researches and they are edited in a comprehensive manner to aid the understanding of the subject.

Apart from the editorial board, the designing team has also invested a significant amount of their time in understanding the subject and creating the most relevant covers. They scrutinized every image to scout for the most suitable representation of the subject and create an appropriate cover for the book.

The publishing team has been involved in this book since its early stages. They were actively engaged in every process, be it collecting the data, connecting with the contributors or procuring relevant information. The team has been an ardent support to the editorial, designing and production team. Their endless efforts to recruit the best for this project, has resulted in the accomplishment of this book. They are a veteran in the field of academics and their pool of knowledge is as vast as their experience in printing. Their expertise and guidance has proved useful at every step. Their uncompromising quality standards have made this book an exceptional effort. Their encouragement from time to time has been an inspiration for everyone.

The publisher and the editorial board hope that this book will prove to be a valuable piece of knowledge for researchers, students, practitioners and scholars across the globe.

List of Contributors

Ammar Babiker and Nordin Zakaria
PETRONAS University of Technology, Malaysia

E. López-Morillo, F. Márquez, T. Sánchez-Rodríguez, C.I. Luján-Martínez and F. Munoz
Electronics Engineering Department, Universidad de Sevilla, Spain

Zhen Gao
Tsinghua University, Tsinghua Research Institute of Information Technology, Tsinghua National Laboratory for Information Science and Technology, P.R. China

Mary Ann Ingram
Georgia Institute of Technology, USA

Kuo-Chang Ting, Hwang-Cheng Wang, Fang-Chang Kuo, Chih-Cheng Tseng and Ping Ho Ting
Minghsin University of Science and Technology, National Ilan University, National Chi Nan University, Taiwan

Sameh Gobriel, Christian Maciocco and Tsung-Yuan Charlie Tai
Circuits and Systems Research Lab, Intel Labs, Intel Corporation, USA

I. Foche, M. Chidean, F.J. Simó-Reigadas, I. Mora-Jiménez, J.L. Rojo-Álvarez, J. Ramiro-Bargueno and A.J. Caamano
Signal Theory and Communications Dept., ETSIT, Rey Juan Carlos University, Madrid, Spain

Printed in the USA
CPSIA information can be obtained
at www.ICGtesting.com
JSHW011333221024
72173JS00003B/143